AVENUES 1
English Skills

Second Edition

LYNNE GAETZ

PEARSON

Montréal Toronto Boston Columbus Indianapolis New York San Francisco Upper Saddle River
Amsterdam Le Cap Dubaï Londres Madrid Milan Munich Paris
Delhi México São Paulo Sydney Hong-Kong Séoul Singapour Taipei Tōkyō

Product Owner
Stephan Leduc

Editor
Lucie Turcotte

Copy Editor
Mairi MacKinnon

Proofreader
Sheryl Curtis

Coordinator, Rights and Permissions
Pierre Richard Bernier

Art Director
Hélène Cousineau

Graphic Design Coordinator
Estelle Cuillerier

Book Design and Layout
Cyclone Design Communications

Cover Design
Frédérique Bouvier

The publisher wishes to thank the many people who provided helpful comments and suggestions throughout the development of this book. Among these, mention goes to the following:

Diane Boisvert, Cégep de Saint-Laurent
Sandra Gasparini, Collège de Bois-de-Boulogne
Barry Glebe, Collège de Maisonneuve
Acsha Ramadeen, Collège de Valleyfield
Raquel Trentin, Cégep de Saint-Jérôme
Heather Yorston, Collège Lionel-Groulx

Cover Photo © plainpicture/Simply North/Frank Chmura

ERPI publishes and distributes PEARSON ELT products in Canada.

1611 Crémazie Boulevard East, 10th Floor
Montréal (Québec) H2M 2P2
CANADA
Telephone: 1 800 263-3678
Fax: 514 334-4720
information@pearsonerpi.com
pearsonerpi.com

Registration of copyright – Bibliothèque et Archives nationales du Québec, 2016
Registration of copyright – Library and Archives Canada, 2016

Printed in Canada 123456789 II 19 18 17 16
ISBN 978-2-7613-6785-1 136785 ABCD ENV94

Acknowledgements
I would like to express sincere thanks to

- Lucie Turcotte for her magnificent job of polishing this book;
- Stephan Leduc and Sharnee Chait for their gentle prodding and valuable expertise;
- Mairi MacKinnon and Sheryl Curtis for their careful work on the manuscript and proofs;
- Hélène Cousineau, Estelle Cuillerier and Cyclone Design for the creative layout;
- My students and colleagues at College Lionel-Groulx for their insightful feedback;
- Rebeka Pelaez and Eileithyia Marshall for their creative contributions;
- Diego Pelaez and Natasha Forgues for their valuable contributions to the website.

I dedicate this book to my life partner, Murray Marshall. He has provided invaluable emotional support over the past years and has helped me feel happy and whole again.

Text Credits

Chapter 1, p. 8 Audio text "Internal Clock" © Canadian Broadcasting Corporation. pp. 10-11 "How to Change Bad Habits" by Aaron Hutchings reprinted by permission. p. 14 Video segment "Home - Part 1" © Lonely Planet; video segment "Home - Part 2" © Mathieu Favreau. pp. 15-16 "The Trouble with Adulthood" reprinted by permission of Barbara Ray, president, HiredPen Inc.—"Research well told."

Chapter 2, pp. 22-23 "My Panick Attacks" reprinted by permission of Rohan Healy, author and musician from Ireland. p. 25 Video segment "Living in Denmark" © ABC News. pp. 31-32 "The Truth about Happiness" by Frank T. McAndrew reprinted by permission. p. 35 Video segment "Meditation and Its Effects on the Brain" © ABC News.

Chapter 3, p. 42 Video segment "Fake Online Reviews" © ABC News. p. 44 Audio text "Generic Brands" © Age of Persuasion; courtesy of Terry O'Reilly. pp. 45-46 "The Compulsive Shopper" reprinted by permission of Rebeka Pelaez. p. 48 Video segment "Damn Heels" © Canadian Broadcasting Corporation. pp. 49-50 "The Sharing Economy" by Terry O'Reilly reprinted by permission. p. 51 Video segment "Consumer Power" © Canadian Broadcasting Corporation.

Chapter 4, p. 58 Video segment "Memory Wizards" © CBS News. pp. 60-61 "Why Childhood Memories Disappear" by Alasdair Wilkins reprinted by permission. p. 67 Video segment "Humans of New York" © CBS News.

Chapter 5, p. 80 Video segment "Gringo Trails," a film by Pegi Vail, courtesy of Icarus Films. pp. 87-88 "Laughing through the Fog" by Eileithyia Marshall reprinted by permission. p. 89 Video segment "Rip Currents" © ABC News.

Chapter 6, pp. 94-96 "Adrenaline Adventures" reprinted by permission; © Originally published on World Travel Guide (www.worldtravelguide.net). p. 98 Video segment "Extreme Climber" © ABC News. pp. 99-100 "BMX Rider: Interview with Kara Bruce" used by permission of Kara Bruce. p. 102 Audio text "Lost in the Wild" © Canadian Broadcasting Corporation. pp. 103-104 "The Rules of Survival" by Laurence Gonzales reprinted from *Deep Survival: Who Lives, Who Dies, and Why*. W.W. Norton. Copyright © 2003 by Laurence Gonzales. Used by permission. p. 105 Video segment "Survival Skills - Part 1: How to Survive a Tornado" © ABC News. p. 106 Video segment "Survival Skills - Part 2: How to Survive a Car Crash through Ice" © ABC News. pp. 106-107 "A Lesson in Brave Parenting" © 2010 reprinted by permission of the author.

Chapter 7, p. 117 Video segment "Distracted Drivers" © Canadian Broadcasting Corporation. pp 118-119 "Your Social Life Is Not Your Social Media" by Peggy Drexler, PhD reprinted by permission. p. 120 Video segment "The Power of Online Shaming" © Canadian Broadcasting Corporation. p. 129 Audio text "Finding Love Online" © Canadian Broadcasting Corporation.

This book is printed on paper made in Québec from 100% post-consumer recycled materials, processed chlorine-free, certified Eco-Logo, and manufactured using biogas energy.

PREFACE

Avenues 1: English Skills is the first of a three-level series. Designed for high-beginner and low-intermediate students of English as a Second Language, *Avenues 1* is a comprehensive integrated skills book. It is also the culmination of my writing career.

In the 1990s, I looked at existing textbooks with integrated grammar blurbs. As an anglophone who moved to Québec, I was aware that a strong background in grammatical concepts helped me feel more secure as I learned French. Thus, when I wrote *Brass Tacks*, I separated the comprehensive grammar section from the skills. Over the years, as I reworked that basic model, I have tried to make the grammar exercises more appealing, and link them more closely to the skills themes. I have also honed my understanding of the types of errors students make, creating skills and grammar content that better matches their needs. Finally, with each new series and edition, I have relished the challenge of researching and finding interesting and relevant material for both students and teachers.

As I developed this second edition of *Avenues 1: English Skills*, I weighed teachers' suggestions. Each chapter now begins with a Quick Chat activity. At the start of class, students can engage in non-stop talking or free-writing to warm up for the day's lessons. In the previous edition, information about reading strategies was scattered throughout the book. The reading strategies have now been consolidated in a section of their own, and students can practise specific ones in a dedicated section of My eLab. For students who struggle with basic vocabulary, My eLab contains a new Basic Vocabulary section. And for students who require more challenge, most chapters contain a difficult reading with a Reading Challenge label. All chapters have a Reading with Listening essay; students can listen and read along, noticing intonation and pronunciation. If students have particular difficulties with reading and listening tests, they can also practise by doing some of the extra exercises available online.

This edition incorporates updated readings, audios, and videos. Three new chapters deal with memories, risk-taking and survival, and life online. The remaining chapters include thought-provoking new reading and video content. Furthermore, testing material has been updated. And if you want to tweak existing tests or develop your own, My eLab provides you with the possibility of adapting, adding, or removing test questions.

Avenues 1: English Skills, Second Edition contains more material than necessary for a forty-five-hour course, allowing you to choose from different chapters once you've exhausted certain topics. Additionally, chapters can be presented in whatever sequence you prefer.

With clear explanations and exercises that complement the themes in the skills component, *Avenues 1: English Grammar*, Second Edition is the perfect companion to this book. If students have particular difficulties with a grammatical concept, they can try additional exercises in My eLab.

Thanks to all of you who have used my series over the years. Best of luck in the coming semester.

Lynne Gaetz

HIGHLIGHTS

Warm-up activities provide a relevant introduction to each chapter, starting with a Quick Chat activity that gets students talking or writing about theme-related topics.

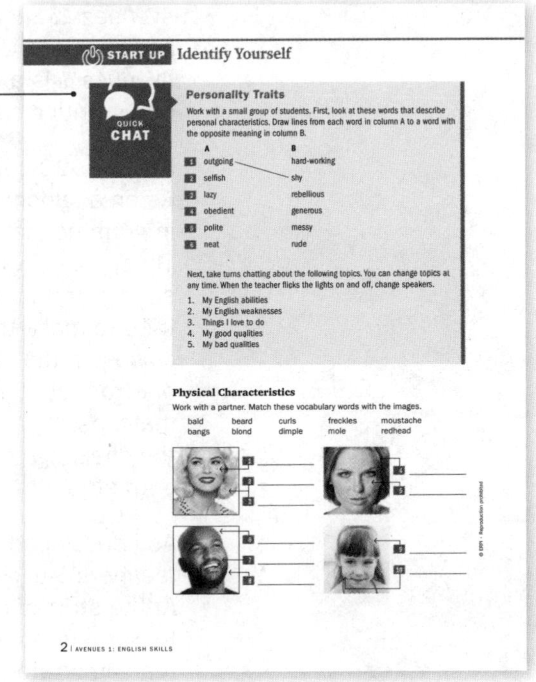
START UP Identify Yourself

QUICK CHAT

Personality Traits

Work with a small group of students. First, look at these words that describe personal characteristics. Draw lines from each word in column A to a word with the opposite meaning in column B.

	A	B
1	outgoing	hard-working
2	selfish	shy
3	lazy	rebellious
4	obedient	generous
5	polite	messy
6	neat	rude

Next, take turns chatting about the following topics. You can change topics at any time. When the teacher flicks the lights on and off, change speakers.

1. My English abilities
2. My English weaknesses
3. Things I love to do
4. My good qualities
5. My bad qualities

Physical Characteristics

Work with a partner. Match these vocabulary words with the images.

bald bangs beard blond curls dimple freckles mole moustache redhead

2 | AVENUES 1: ENGLISH SKILLS

Audio and video segments offer a range of rich listening practice material.

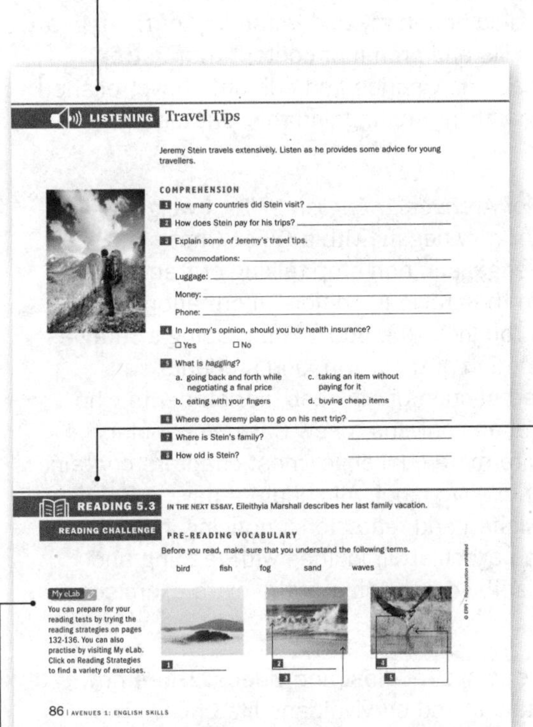
LISTENING Travel Tips

Jeremy Stein travels extensively. Listen as he provides some advice for young travellers.

COMPREHENSION

1. How many countries did Stein visit?
2. How does Stein pay for his trips?
3. Explain some of Jeremy's travel tips.
   Accommodations:
   Luggage:
   Money:
   Phone:
4. In Jeremy's opinion, should you buy health insurance?
   ☐ Yes ☐ No
5. What is *haggling*?
   a. going back and forth while negotiating a final price
   b. eating with your fingers
   c. taking an item without paying for it
   d. buying cheap items
6. Where does Jeremy plan to go on his next trip?
7. Where is Stein's family?
8. How old is Stein?

READING 5.3 IN THE NEXT ESSAY, Eleithyia Marshall describes her last family vacation.

READING CHALLENGE

PRE-READING VOCABULARY

Before you read, make sure that you understand the following terms.

bird fish fog sand waves

My eLab: You can prepare for your reading tests by trying the reading strategies on pages 132-136. You can also practise by visiting My eLab. Click on Reading Strategies to find a variety of exercises.

86 | AVENUES 1: ENGLISH SKILLS

Texts taken from a variety of sources expose students to different writing styles and ideas.

Vocabulary Boosts help students build their vocabulary by examining the different nuances between commonly confused words.

My eLab contains additional questions for the book's reading and listening activities, extra material for further comprehension practice, as well as vocabulary and reading strategy practice exercises.

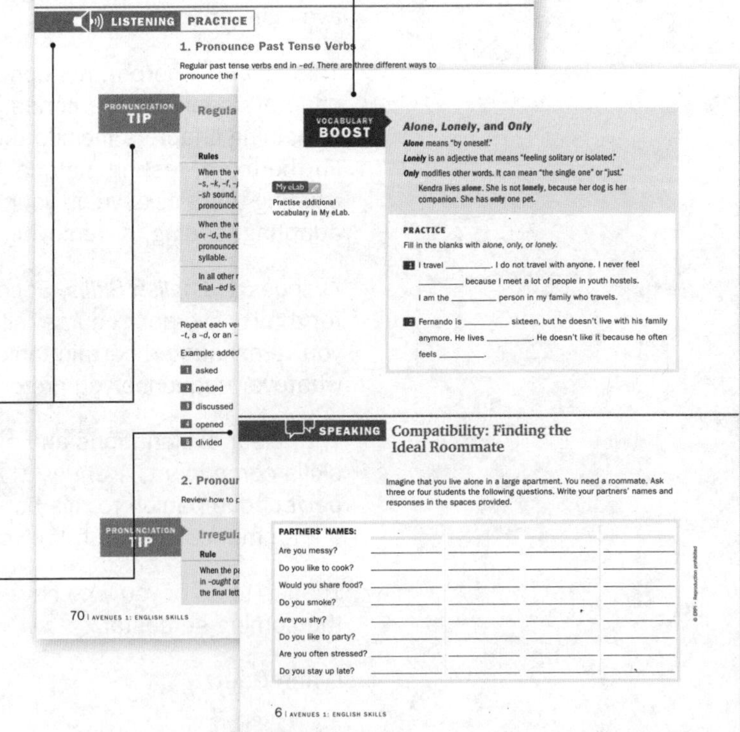
LISTENING PRACTICE

1. Pronounce Past Tense Verbs

Regular past tense verbs end in *-ed*. There are three different ways to pronounce the f…

PRONUNCIATION TIP

Repeat each ve… -t, a -d, or an -…

Example: added

1. asked
2. needed
3. discussed
4. opened
5. divided

2. Pronour…

PRONUNCIATION TIP

70 | AVENUES 1: ENGLISH SKILLS

VOCABULARY BOOST

Alone, Lonely, and Only

Alone means "by oneself."

Lonely is an adjective that means "feeling solitary or isolated."

Only modifies other words. It can mean "the single one" or "just."

Kendra lives ***alone***. She is not ***lonely***, because her dog is her companion. She has ***only*** one pet.

My eLab: Practise additional vocabulary in My eLab.

PRACTICE

Fill in the blanks with *alone*, *only*, or *lonely*.

1. I travel ______. I do not travel with anyone. I never feel ______ because I meet a lot of people in youth hostels. I am the ______ person in my family who travels.
2. Fernando is ______ sixteen, but he doesn't live with his family anymore. He lives ______. He doesn't like it because he often feels ______.

SPEAKING Compatibility: Finding the Ideal Roommate

Imagine that you live alone in a large apartment. You need a roommate. Ask three or four students the following questions. Write your partners' names and responses in the spaces provided.

PARTNERS' NAMES:				
Are you messy?				
Do you like to cook?				
Would you share food?				
Do you smoke?				
Are you shy?				
Do you like to party?				
Are you often stressed?				
Do you stay up late?				

6 | AVENUES 1: ENGLISH SKILLS

Exercises and useful tips allow students to practise pronunciation.

Speaking activities particularly emphasize question formation.

In each chapter, the Take Action! section includes additional writing and speaking topics, as well as presentation topics.

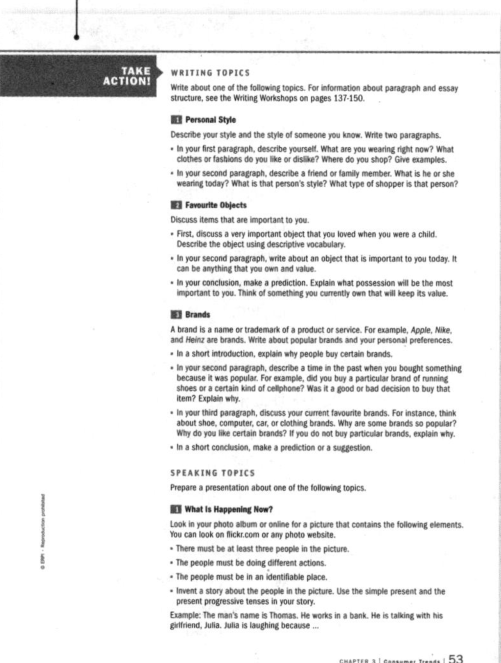

TAKE ACTION!

WRITING TOPICS

Write about one of the following topics. For information about paragraph and essay structure, see the Writing Workshops on pages 137-150.

1 Personal Style

Describe your style and the style of someone you know. Write two paragraphs.

- In your first paragraph, describe yourself. What are you wearing right now? What clothes or fashions do you like or dislike? Where do you shop? Give examples.
- In your second paragraph, describe a friend or family member. What is he or she wearing today? What is that person's style? What type of shopper is that person?

2 Favourite Objects

Discuss items that are important to you.

- First, discuss a very important object that you loved when you were a child. Describe the object using descriptive vocabulary.
- In your second paragraph, write about an object that is important to you today. It can be anything that you own and value.
- In your conclusion, make a prediction. Explain what possession will be the most important to you. Think of something you currently own that will keep its value.

3 Brands

A brand is a name or trademark of a product or service. For example, *Apple*, *Nike*, and *Heinz* are brands. Write about popular brands and your personal preferences.

- In a short introduction, explain why people buy certain brands.
- In your second paragraph, describe a time in the past when you bought something because it was popular. For example, did you buy a particular brand of running shoes or a certain kind of cellphone? Was it a good or bad decision to buy that item? Explain why.
- In your third paragraph, discuss your current favourite brands. For instance, think about shoe, computer, car, or clothing brands. Why are some brands so popular? Why do you like certain brands? If you do not buy particular brands, explain why.
- In a short conclusion, make a prediction or a suggestion.

SPEAKING TOPICS

Prepare a presentation about one of the following topics.

1 What Is Happening Now?

Look in your photo album or online for a picture that contains the following elements. You can look on flickr.com or any photo website.

- There must be at least three people in the picture.
- The people must be doing different actions.
- The people must be in an identifiable place.
- Invent a story about the people in the picture. Use the simple present and the present progressive tenses in your story.

Example: The man's name is Thomas. He works in a bank. He is talking with his girlfriend, Julia. Julia is laughing because ...

The Revising and Editing section helps students develop their writing skills and prepare for writing tests, including TESOL tests.

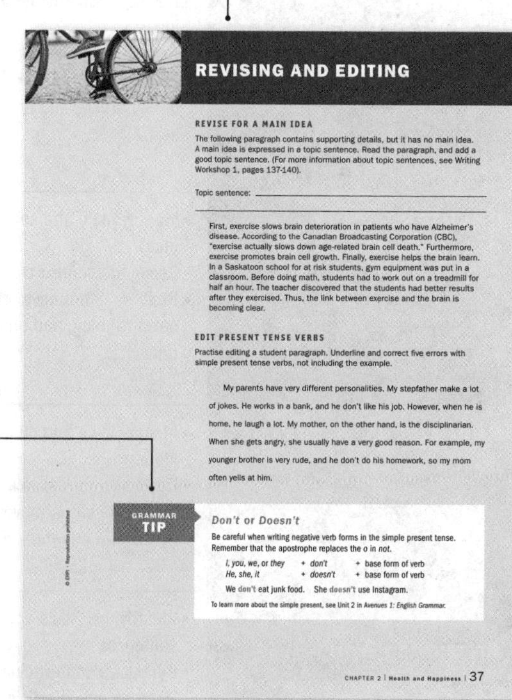

REVISING AND EDITING

REVISE FOR A MAIN IDEA

The following paragraph contains supporting details, but it has no main idea. A main idea is expressed in a topic sentence. Read the paragraph, and add a good topic sentence. (For more information about topic sentences, see Writing Workshop 1, pages 137-140).

Topic sentence: ______________________

First, exercise slows brain deterioration in patients who have Alzheimer's disease. According to the Canadian Broadcasting Corporation (CBC), "exercise actually slows down age-related brain cell death." Furthermore, exercise promotes brain cell growth. Finally, exercise helps the brain learn. In a Saskatoon school for at risk students, gym equipment was put in a classroom. Before doing math, students had to work out on a treadmill for half an hour. The teacher discovered that the students had better results after they exercised. Thus, the link between exercise and the brain is becoming clear.

EDIT PRESENT TENSE VERBS

Practise editing a student paragraph. Underline and correct five errors with simple present tense verbs, not including the example.

My parents have very different personalities. My stepfather make a lot of jokes. He works in a bank, and he don't like his job. However, when he is home, he laugh a lot. My mother, on the other hand, is the disciplinarian. When she gets angry, she usually have a very good reason. For example, my younger brother is very rude, and he don't do his homework, so my mom often yells at him.

GRAMMAR TIP

Don't or *Doesn't*

Be careful when writing negative verb forms in the simple present tense. Remember that the apostrophe replaces the *o* in *not*.

I, you, we, or *they* + *don't* + base form of verb
He, she, it + *doesn't* + base form of verb

We don't eat junk food. She doesn't use Instagram.

To learn more about the simple present, see Unit 2 in *Avenues 1: English Grammar*.

Throughout the book, Grammar Tips cover key concepts that are further explored in *Avenues 1: English Grammar*.

WRITING WORKSHOP 1
WRITING A PARAGRAPH

Generating Ideas

READING STRATEGIES

My eLab: Visit My eLab for more practice trying the different reading strategies.

My eLab: Visit My eLab for more practice using context clues.

Vocabulary

When you read, you expand your vocabulary and you learn how English writers develop ideas. Review the following tips. Note that you can practise these strategies online in My eLab.

Recognizing Context Clues

When you read a document and come across a new word, what do you do? If you constantly have to use a dictionary or glossary, it can slow down your reading and make you feel frustrated. But if you skip over difficult words, you might not understand what you read.

An effective way to determine a word's meaning is to use context clues. Context clues are hints that help clarify a word's meaning. Look for context clues in a text by following these steps:

1. Look at the parts of the word. You might recognize a part of the word and be able to guess the meaning (hairdresser).
2. Determine the part of speech. Sometimes it helps to know a word's function. Is it a noun, a verb, an adjective, and so on? For example, *His night shift ended at 8 a.m.* You know that *shift* is a noun. This can help you guess its meaning.
3. Look at surrounding words and sentences. Look for a synonym (a word that has the same meaning) or an antonym (a word that has the opposite meaning). Also look at surrounding sentences, and use logic to deduce, or guess, the word's meaning.

PRACTICE 1

1. Determine the meaning of the words in bold.

a. Some consumers buy **trendy** clothes. Two months later, the trend is over and the fashion item is relegated to the bottom of the closet.

Part of speech: a. adjective b. noun c. verb

Clue: ______________________

Meaning: ______________________

b. Mr. and Mrs. Perez are extremely excited because their business is **booming**! They have more customers every day.

Part of speech: a. adjective b. noun c. verb

Clue: ______________________

Meaning: ______________________

Three Writing Workshops provide detailed explanations on paragraph development, essay structure, and revising techniques.

The Reading Strategies section highlights concepts that help students improve their reading skills. Online practice prepares them for reading tests, including TESOL tests.

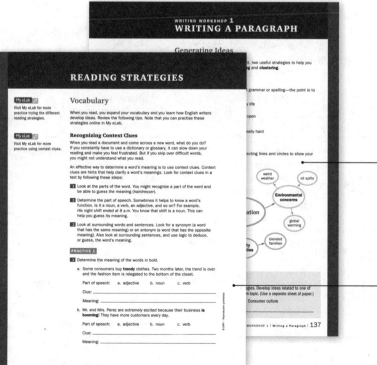

SCOPE AND SEQUENCE

	READING	WRITING	LISTENING/WATCHING
CHAPTER 1 **Self-Reflections**	▪ Identify main and supporting ideas ▪ Read a narrative blog, a "how-to" article, and an opinion text	▪ Write simple present (third-person singular) sentences ▪ Analyze character and motives ▪ Write paragraphs on habits and values ▪ Edit a paragraph	▪ Listen for pronouns ▪ Listen to phone messages ▪ Listen for main ideas ▪ Listen to a reading text ▪ Listen to an interview on lateness ▪ Watch videos on the meaning of home
CHAPTER 2 **Health and Happiness**	▪ Identify main and supporting ideas ▪ Recognize context clues ▪ Read a narrative blog, an online article, and an opinion essay	▪ Write about health and lifestyle ▪ Brainstorm ideas ▪ Write a topic sentence ▪ Practise the simple present ▪ Write interview questions ▪ Edit a paragraph	▪ Listen to verbs ending in *–s* or *–es* ▪ Listen to a reading text ▪ Watch a video about living in Denmark ▪ Watch a video on meditation effects
CHAPTER 3 **Consumer Trends**	▪ Identify main and supporting ideas ▪ Recognize context clues ▪ Read an informative article, a narrative blog, and an audio transcript	▪ Write about consumer culture ▪ Write interview questions ▪ Summarize main ideas ▪ Write a paragraph based on a partner's responses ▪ Use transition words ▪ Edit a paragraph	▪ Watch videos about fake online reviews and consumer power ▪ Watch *Dragon's Den* ▪ Listen to large numbers and verb pronunciation ▪ Listen to a reading text ▪ Listen to "Generic Brands"
CHAPTER 4 **Memories of Our Lives**	▪ Identify main and supporting ideas ▪ Read an informative article and personal narratives ▪ Synthesize information	▪ Write about your childhood ▪ Write present and past questions ▪ Write supporting details ▪ Edit a paragraph	▪ Listen for main ideas ▪ Listen to a reading text ▪ Watch *Memory Wizards* and *Humans of New York* ▪ Listen to an interview about the 1990s
CHAPTER 5 **Around the World**	▪ Identify the thesis and topic sentences ▪ Recognize context clues ▪ Read an online article, an informative article, and a personal narrative	▪ Write an introduction ▪ Write questions and definitions ▪ Write about travel ▪ Write about a partner's responses ▪ Edit an essay	▪ Listen for main and supporting ideas ▪ Listen to details on prices, dates, and places ▪ Listen to directions ▪ Listen to travel tips ▪ Watch videos on travel and riptides
CHAPTER 6 **Risk-Taking and Survival**	▪ Identify the message ▪ Read online articles, an interview, and a book excerpt ▪ Identify main idea and details ▪ Recognize context clues ▪ Do team-reading	▪ Practise dictation ▪ Write questions and definitions ▪ Summarize information ▪ Write about risk-taking ▪ Write a conclusion ▪ Edit an essay	▪ Listen for main ideas and details ▪ Identify silent letters ▪ Listen to an interview on survival ▪ Watch videos on extreme climbing and survival skills
CHAPTER 7 **Life Online**	▪ Respond to a text ▪ Identify main and supporting ideas ▪ Read an online article and a short story ▪ Identify the message	▪ Write present, past, and future questions ▪ Write comparisons ▪ Write about social media and addictions ▪ Support opinions	▪ Pronounce *t* and *th* ▪ Listen for main and supporting ideas ▪ Listen to an interview on online dating ▪ Watch videos on online shaming and texting while driving

SPEAKING	VOCABULARY	GRAMMAR	REVISING AND EDITING
▪ Make introductions ▪ Share information on habits, attitudes, and compatibility ▪ Interview a partner ▪ Pronounce pronouns and sentences ▪ Present oral topics	▪ Learn personal identification terms ▪ Learn verbs related to habits ▪ Vocabulary Boosts: *alone*, *lonely*, *only*; telling the time	▪ Form questions ▪ Learn capitalization rules ▪ Write birthdates ▪ Use third-person singular subjects ▪ Identify pronoun errors	▪ Revise for adequate support ▪ Edit for pronoun usage
▪ Use question words ▪ Discuss health and internal organs ▪ Interview a partner ▪ Pronounce verbs ending in *-s* ▪ Pronounce sentences	▪ Practise question words ▪ Learn emotion vocabulary ▪ Vocabulary Boosts: body parts; *fun*, *funny* and *humour*	▪ Use question words ▪ Practise subject-verb agreement and present and past tenses ▪ Use adjectives ▪ Identify present tense errors	▪ Revise for main idea (add a topic sentence) ▪ Edit for present tense verbs
▪ Interview a partner about fashion trends ▪ Ask questions ▪ Discuss clothing ▪ Present past, present, and future trends	▪ Describe trends ▪ Vocabulary Boost: *for sale*, *on sale*, and *sell* ▪ Learn clothing vocabulary ▪ Identify numbers	▪ Use present, present progressive, and future verbs ▪ Use adjectives ▪ Form questions ▪ Identify progressive verb errors	▪ Revise for transitional expressions ▪ Edit for present progressive verbs
▪ Play memory games ▪ Discuss birth order and memories ▪ Pronounce past verbs and sentences ▪ Speak about a life-changing event	▪ Vocabulary Boosts: *remember*, *memory, souvenir* and *memoir*; family members ▪ Learn two-word expressions	▪ Form past questions ▪ Identify past verbs ▪ View verbs in context ▪ Identify past verb errors	▪ Revise for supporting details ▪ Edit for past tense verbs
▪ Name countries ▪ Interview a partner about travel ▪ Ask questions in a variety of tenses ▪ Discuss gestures	▪ Discuss travel plans ▪ Learn about countries and nationalities ▪ Vocabulary Boost: travel terms ▪ Learn vocabulary related to gestures and directions	▪ Form questions ▪ Use *the* ▪ Use *will* ▪ Identify modal and verb errors Practise present, past, and future tenses	▪ Revise for an introduction ▪ Edit for modals
▪ Discuss extreme sports ▪ Discuss parenting rules ▪ Pronounce words with silent letters ▪ Interview a role model	▪ Use action verbs and adjectives ▪ Vocabulary Boosts: *make*, *do*, *play*, and *go*; *let*, *leave* ▪ Learn bike parts ▪ Use comparative adjectives	▪ Use modals ▪ Form questions ▪ Give advice ▪ Practise tenses ▪ Make comparisons ▪ Identify plural errors	▪ Revise for a conclusion ▪ Edit for plural and comparative form errors
▪ Discuss apps and social media ▪ Discuss present and past technology ▪ Discuss a short story and share ideas ▪ Pronounce *t* and *th* ▪ Discuss online dating	▪ Vocabulary Boost: technology ▪ Use comparative adjectives ▪ Make guesses on word meanings	▪ Give commands ▪ Practise question forms ▪ Use modals ▪ Make comparisons	▪ Revise for sentence variety ▪ Edit for mixed errors

TABLE OF CONTENTS

CHAPTER **1**

SELF-REFLECTIONS

"Everyone thinks of changing the world, but no one thinks of changing himself."

— LEO TOLSTOY, RUSSIAN AUTHOR

What do you want to accomplish in life? In this introductory chapter, you will have the opportunity to write about yourself.

START UP Identify Yourself

Personality Traits

Work with a small group of students. First, look at these words that describe personal characteristics. Draw lines from each word in column A to a word with the opposite meaning in column B.

	A	B
1	outgoing	hard-working
2	selfish	shy
3	lazy	rebellious
4	obedient	generous
5	polite	messy
6	neat	rude

Next, take turns chatting about the following topics. You can change topics at any time. When the teacher flicks the lights on and off, change speakers.

1. My English abilities
2. My English weaknesses
3. Things I love to do
4. My good qualities
5. My bad qualities

Physical Characteristics

Work with a partner. Match these vocabulary words with the images.

bald	beard	curls	freckles	moustache
bangs	blond	dimple	mole	redhead

1 ____________

2 ____________

3 ____________

4 ____________

5 ____________

6 ____________

7 ____________

8 ____________

9 ____________

10 ____________

Identification Form

Interview your partner. Complete the form with your partner's answers. To review vocabulary on marital status and titles, see Appendix 2 on page 152.

IDENTIFICATION

Name: Last ______________ First ______________ Middle ______________

Title (choose one): ☐ Mr. ☐ Miss ☐ Mrs. ☐ Ms.

Birthplace: ____________________ **Eye colour:** ____________________

Birthdate: ____________________ **Hair colour:** ____________________

Marital status (choose one):

☐ Single ☐ Married

☐ Separated ☐ Divorced

☐ Common law ☐ Widowed

Distinguishing features:

☐ Mole ☐ Dimples

☐ Tattoo ☐ Piercing

Other:

Citizenship: ____

WRITING

Write one paragraph about yourself and a second paragraph about your partner. Use information from the identification form.

GRAMMAR TIP

Age, Birthplace, and Birthdate

Age

Use *be* to state your age. Do not use *have*.

How old **are** you? I **am** seventeen years old, and my brother **is** twenty.

Birthplace

Describe where you were born using the past tense of *be* + *born*.

Where **were you** born? I **was born** in Halifax.

Birthdate

Use *on* + month + day. Capitalize the month.

Jeff's birthday is **on March 21**.

Note: You can also say "Jeff's birthday is **on the 21st of March**."

For more information about prepositions, see Unit 9 in *Avenues 1: English Grammar.*

My eLab

Visit My eLab for practice in pronouncing and identifying names, ages, and birthdates. You might review the English pronunciation of letters of the alphabet.

COULD ALEXIS AND DOMINIQUE live together as roommates? Work with a partner. One of you can read Alexis's answers, and the other can read Dominique's answers. Then decide if they are compatible.

My eLab

You can prepare for your reading tests by trying the reading strategies on pages 132-136. You can also practise by visiting My eLab. Click on Reading Strategies to find a variety of exercises.

Roommate Hunt: Are They Compatible?

1 Describe your character.

ALEXIS

My name is Alexis, but people call me Lex for short. I am casual and **down to earth**. I am **super chill** about most things. You usually see me in a T-shirt and jeans, and in the summer I wear flip-flops. I have some health issues. I am really allergic to animal fur and dust. I sometimes have asthma attacks if I'm in a place that is dirty.

DOMINIQUE

My name is Dominique, but my friends call me Dom. I am serious and hard-working. I have a busy life because I work thirty hours a week and I also go to college. People tell me that I am **high-strung**. When I am home, I need to relax. I usually **hang out** with my dogs, Pete and Rex, after work.

2 What is your daily schedule like?

ALEXIS

On weekdays, I take college classes. The campus is nearby, so I can usually wake up at 8 or 9 a.m. It depends on my class schedule. I usually go to sleep at about midnight. On weekends, I stay up really late, until 2 or 3 a.m., and then sleep in. I am, by nature, a **night owl**.

DOMINIQUE

I work in a marketing agency, and I take the subway to work. On weekdays, I wake up at 6 a.m. and leave the house by 7 a.m. I try to get to bed by 10 p.m. every night. During the weekend, I like to read, **work out** at the gym, and sometimes have dinners with friends. I rarely stay up past midnight.

3 What are your strongest beliefs?

ALEXIS

I am open-minded and optimistic. I am interested in Buddhism, and I also have a strong belief in astrology. I'm a Capricorn, and I know how to read astrological charts. I like serious discussions, but I hate talking about politics.

DOMINIQUE

I have strong political beliefs. I hate the current government, and I love intelligent debates about politics. I don't care about celebrity culture, and I don't watch dumb TV shows. Also, I don't believe in God. I am an atheist.

4 Describe your living environment.

ALEXIS

My apartment is very tidy. I am a little compulsive about cleanliness. If you saw my clothes closet, you would notice that my clothing is organized according to colour and season. I hate a dirty kitchen, so I wash up after every meal. I like a very tidy home, probably because of my allergies.

DOMINIQUE

Well, I have two dogs, so my place is a little **messy**. There is fur everywhere. I don't have time to do laundry, so I admit that there are piles of clothes here and there. Sometimes, about once a month, I tidy up, but usually my place looks chaotic. I like it that way.

ALEXIS	DOMINIQUE
5 **What is your worst habit?**	
Hmm, I spend too much time online. I love reality shows like *The Voice*, so I **binge-watch** a lot of television series online.	I smoke. I would like to stop, but right now my life is pretty stressful. I will stop one day.

(494 words)

COMPREHENSION

COMMON EXPRESSIONS

1 Guess the meanings of the expressions in bold. Don't use a dictionary. Instead, look at the words in context and make a guess. (For more information about context clues, see pages 132-133.)

1. down to earth: ____________________
2. super chill: ____________________
3. high-strung: ____________________
4. hang out: ____________________
5. night owl: ____________________
6. work out: ____________________
7. messy: ____________________
8. binge-watch: ____________________

2 Which person, in your opinion, is very *laid-back*? (*Laid-back* means "relaxed, easy to get along with.")

____

3 Which person, in your opinion, is *edgy*? (*Edgy* means "nervous and tense, and maybe a little harsh.")

____

My eLab

Answer additional reading and listening questions in My eLab. You can also access audio and video clips online.

DISCUSSION AND WRITING

Are Alexis and Dominique compatible? Would they be good roommates? Why or why not? Write a paragraph explaining your point of view.

GRAMMAR TIP

Third-Person Singular Subjects

When you describe another person's habits, remember to put an -s or -es at the end of each verb. Add *does not* to negative forms.

She **watches** a lot of television shows. He **does not smoke**.

To learn more about the simple present, see Unit 2 in *Avenues 1: English Grammar.*

VOCABULARY BOOST

Alone, Lonely, and *Only*

Alone means "by oneself."

Lonely is an adjective that means "feeling solitary or isolated."

Only modifies other words. It can mean "the single one" or "just."

Kendra lives **alone**. She is not **lonely**, because her dog is her companion. She has **only** one pet.

My eLab

Practise additional vocabulary in My eLab.

PRACTICE

Fill in the blanks with *alone*, *only*, or *lonely*.

1 I travel __________. I do not travel with anyone. I never feel __________ because I meet a lot of people in youth hostels. I am the __________ person in my family who travels.

2 Fernando is __________ sixteen, but he doesn't live with his family anymore. He lives __________. He doesn't like it because he often feels __________.

SPEAKING Compatibility: Finding the Ideal Roommate

Imagine that you live alone in a large apartment. You need a roommate. Ask three or four students the following questions. Write your partners' names and responses in the spaces provided.

PARTNERS' NAMES:				
Are you messy?				
Do you like to cook?				
Would you share food?				
Do you smoke?				
Are you shy?				
Do you like to party?				
Are you often stressed?				
Do you stay up late?				

WRITING

Write ten sentences. Explain whom you are compatible with and who is not compatible with you. Explain why.

Example: Sayid and I are compatible. He doesn't smoke, and I don't smoke.

LISTENING PRACTICE

1. Pronounce Pronouns

Repeat each sentence after the speaker. Then fill in the missing pronoun or possessive adjective.

Example: Karen found her wallet.

1 Karen often loses ______________ purse.

2 Today, she doesn't know where ______________ keys are.

3 Her husband has ______________ own bad habits.

4 Mr. Henry Hall always bites ______________ pens and pencils.

5 At work, he often sings when ______________ is bored.

6 His colleagues sometimes laugh at ______________.

7 Henry and Karen don't spend time with ______________ children.

8 They rarely take care of ______________.

9 My brother and I sometimes lie to ______________ parents.

10 What are ______________ bad habits?

2. Take Telephone Messages

You will hear two telephone conversations. Complete the information in each memo.

CALL 1

Doctor's Appointment

Name: ______________

Medicare number: ______________

Date of appointment: ______________

Time of appointment: ______________

Reason for appointment: ______________

CALL 2

Job Application

Title (underline one): Mr. / Miss / Mrs. / Ms.

First name: ______________

Initial: ___ Last name: ______________

Marital status (choose one):
☐ Single ☐ Married ☐ Common law ☐ Widowed

Birthdate: February 23, ______________

Street Address: ________ Rice Avenue

City: __________, Alberta Postal Code: ________

Phone number: ______________

LISTENING Internal Clock

Your internal clock determines when you sleep and wake up. It also influences how you perceive time. Do you make others wait? Are you always late or always early for events? Sook-Yin Lee interviews Sara Tate about her chronic lateness.

Begin by listening to the first part of the interview and completing the vocabulary exercise. Then listen to the rest of the interview and answer the comprehension questions.

VOCABULARY

1 Fill in the blanks with the words that you hear in the first part of the interview.

Lee: When it comes to time, we all perceive it a little differently. But have you ever wondered why some people's internal __________ seems to run a little—or sometimes a lot—behind everyone else's?

Chronically late DNTO producer Sara Tate has managed to make it to the studio __________, and she is here to make a confession and hopefully mend her __________ ways.

Tate: Yes, Sook-Yin: I am punctually challenged. I've missed __________ parties. I've missed flights. I was even late for my own __________.

2 Match the words to their meanings.

Terms		Definitions
1. on time	______	a. diary or notebook to record private thoughts
2. wedding	______	b. time-keeping device
3. journal	______	c. punctual
4. tardy	______	d. ceremony to celebrate a marriage
5. clock	______	e. late

COMPREHENSION

Answer the following questions.

3 What is Sara's main problem? ______________________________

4 What is the name of Sara's husband? ______________________________

5 When did Sara begin to hate waiting? Circle the letter of the correct answer.

a. When she was a little girl

b. When she was in college

c. When she was in junior high school

6 What advice did Diana DeLonzor give Sara? ______________________

____

7 What is Sara never late for?

a. Her job b. Her husband c. Her doctor

8 Why does Sara decide to change her late habit? ______________________

Are the next two sentences true or false? Circle *T* for "true" or *F* for "false."

9 Sara's husband doesn't care that she is always late. T F

10 Diana DeLonzor wrote a book. T F

WRITING

Write a paragraph about lateness. Describe if you are a punctual person or a late person. Explain how you feel when you have to wait for someone. What is your opinion of people who are always late?

VOCABULARY **BOOST**

My eLab

Visit My eLab to try an additional time-telling exercise.

Telling the Time

With digital clocks and watches, people use precise numbers to tell the time. Use *a.m.* in the morning and *p.m.* in the afternoon and evening.

It is **9:36 a.m.**

It is **5:21 p.m.**

Use **o'clock** when it is exactly one o'clock, two o'clock, and so on. You cannot say "two fifteen o'clock." At 12:00 in the daytime, say "**noon**." At 12:00 in the night, say "**midnight**."

With regular clocks and watches, people tell the time using minutes to the hour or minutes after the hour. Note that you don't have to say the word minutes.

to

It is 11:55.

It is five (minutes) to twelve.

past (or **after**)

It is 9:10.

It is ten (minutes) past (or after) nine.

Time can also be divided into quarters or halves.

It is a **quarter** to twelve.

It is **half** past eight.

It is a **quarter** after (or past) twelve.

PRACTICE

Write each time using *to* or *past*.

EXAMPLE: 2:40 It is twenty (minutes) to three.

1 11:15 ______

2 6:30 ______

3 7:10 ______

4 4:20 ______

5 9:50 ______

6 1:45 ______

7 2:25 ______

8 12:00 ______

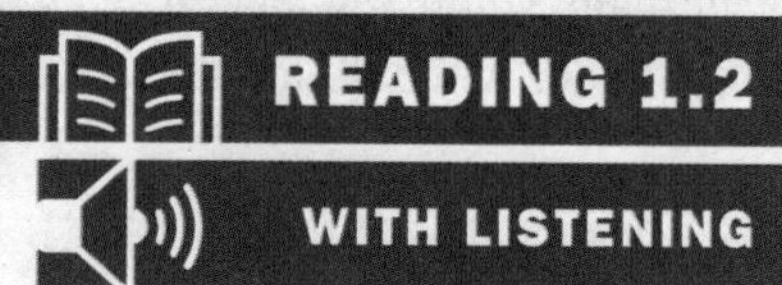

DO YOU HAVE ANY BAD HABITS that you wish you could change? Read about a useful strategy for changing those bad habits.

GRAMMAR LINK

As you read, you will see some pronoun choices in parentheses. Underline or highlight the appropriate pronoun. In My eLab, you can listen to this essay and check your answers. While you are listening, pay attention to the speaker's intonation and pronunciation.

How to Change Bad Habits

BY AARON HUTCHINS

1 After every trip to the bathroom, BJ Fogg gets down on the ground and does two push-ups. Then he washes (his / her / him) hands. It sounds kind of weird, if you stop to think about it, but Fogg doesn't think about it anymore. (It's / Its) a habit he developed to help get in shape. Now, the push-ups come automatically, and he gets a surge of energy each time. Often, he doesn't stop at two. On some trips, he might do ten or twenty-five. "I probably did fifty or sixty push-ups yesterday," he says.

My eLab

You can prepare for your reading tests by trying the reading strategies on pages 132-136. You can also practise by visiting My eLab. Click on Reading Strategies to find a variety of exercises.

2 Fogg is perfectly placed to train (hisself / himself / herself) into a healthy habit. He is the director of the Persuasive Technology Lab. From (his / her / him) research, he learned that the best way to automate a new habit is to set the bar incredibly low. Therefore, he does just two push-ups. "You pick something so small, it's easy to do. Motivation isn't required to do it," he says. Even though he is now much stronger, he says he will never raise the minimum. The goal remains two push-ups, and anything more is a bonus. "If you want to maintain the habit, you will always be okay with just doing the tiny version of it," he says.

3 Studies have shown that approximately 40 to 45 percent of what we do every day is a habit—something we do by default. When we wake up, we brush our teeth. We get in the car to go to work and, without thinking, we put on (our / ours) seatbelts. There's no decision-making and nobody tells (we / us / our) to do it; it's automatic. If almost half the things we do are out of habit, it's a smart plan to make those habits the right ones. Good habits, in effect, can be the prelude to happiness. But developing a good habit, or breaking a bad one, isn't easy, as anyone who has made a New Year's resolution can attest.

trigger: detonator; initiating factor

4 A habit has three components, says Charles Duhigg, a *New York Times* reporter and author of *The Power of Habit*. There's the cue, which is the **trigger** for an automatic behaviour to start. There's the routine, which is the behaviour itself. Last, there's the reward, which is how our brain learns to latch onto that pattern in the future. "When most people think about changing (there / they're / their) habits, they just focus on the behaviour," he says. "What studies have shown is, it's really diagnosing and understanding the cue and the reward that gives people the ability to shift automatic behaviour."

5 Duhigg had a bad habit of going to his work cafeteria every afternoon for a chocolate-chip cookie. The daily snack caused (he / his / him) to put on eight pounds, so he decided to study his craving. It happened consistently around 3 p.m. That was his cue: the time of day. His routine was straightforward. He got up from his desk, went to the cafeteria, grabbed a cookie, and chatted with his colleagues while eating it. Figuring out the reward he was seeking took some trial and error. "Is it that I'm hungry, in which case, eating an apple does the job?" he says. "Or do I need a boost of energy, so coffee should work just as well?" Duhigg tried buying a candy bar and eating it at (his / her / him) desk. He tried going to the cafeteria, buying nothing, but socializing as he normally would. It became clear that the reward was the social time. Now, he'll just get up and chat with a colleague for ten minutes before going back to his desk. The cookie has become a thing of the past.

anchor: key element

6 Little fixes can make a big difference. The key is not to think about grand, sweeping changes, but rather, small ones. Fogg would say very, very small. And be patient. New habits, on average, take sixty-six days to form, according to research from University College London. To build a habit, Fogg says, you use an existing routine, such as brushing (your / you're / our) teeth, as the **anchor**. That anchor becomes the reminder. Next, you do an incredibly simple version of the target behaviour. If you want to develop the habit of flossing, you make (your / you're / our) goal to floss one tooth. That's it. The habit isn't learning how to floss, because everyone knows how to do it. The habit, Fogg says, is remembering to do it. Then, the final step is to celebrate instantly. Maybe shout Victory! "(Your / You're) deliberately firing off an emotion right after you floss. Emotions create habits. The habits that form quickly in our lives have an instant emotional payoff," says Fogg.

(747 words)

Source: Hutchins, Aaron. "The Simple Secrets to Happiness: Turns Out a Better Life Rests on Habits." *Macleans*. Rogers, 27 Feb., 2015. Web. 3 Aug. 2015.

COMPREHENSION

MAIN AND SUPPORTING IDEAS

1 In paragraph 2, the writer says, "the best way to automate a new habit is to set the bar incredibly low." Use your own words to explain what that sentence means.

____

2 About what percentage of our daily activities are habits, or things we do by default?

a. 20 to 25 percent b. 40 to 45 percent c. 60 to 65 percent

3 What are the three parts that make up a habit? See paragraph 4.

______________ ______________ ______________

4 In paragraph 5, what is the meaning of *craving*?

a. terrible event b. breaking a habit c. powerful desire

5 What habit did Charles Duhigg try to develop?

a. doing push-ups every day

b. not eating a cookie every afternoon

c. flossing his teeth every day

6 According to the writer's logic, if you want to develop the habit of eating more vegetables, which step should you take?

a. Eat a salad every day.

b. Fill your fridge mainly with vegetables.

c. Eat one small carrot every day.

7 According to this article, which activities will help you change a habit? Choose four answers.

___ Recognize the stimulus that makes you do something.

___ Make a New Year's resolution to change your bad habit.

___ Recognize the reward you get for doing that activity.

___ Focus on very small changes.

___ Punish yourself every time you engage in that habit.

___ Find a time when you can repeat your habit each day.

GRAMMAR LINK

8 In the first sentence in paragraph 1, what are the two verbs?

______________ ______________

9 In the third sentence in paragraph 1, why does *sounds* end in *–s*?

____

10 What is the negative form of *he stops*? The answer is near the end of paragraph 1. ______________

WRITING

Write about one of your bad habits. Include answers to the following questions:

- What is your bad habit? Explain why that activity or behaviour is bad for you.
- How does that bad habit affect you?
- What is the cue—or initiating factor—that sets off that activity?
- What is your routine? When and where do you perform it?
- What is your reward? What benefits do you get for engaging in that behaviour?
- Propose a solution. What could you do to change that habit?

SPEAKING Good and Bad Habits

Work with a partner. Ask your partner questions to find out about his or her habits. Indicate which habits your partner has or doesn't have.

Partner's name: ____________________________

PERSONAL HABITS **Do you ...**	NEVER	SOMETIMES	OFTEN
make people wait for you?	☐	☐	☐
text while driving?	☐	☐	☐
lie to others?	☐	☐	☐
spend too much time using social media?	☐	☐	☐
wash your dishes after using them?	☐	☐	☐
put items away after using them?	☐	☐	☐
use Facebook, Instagram, or other social networking sites?	☐	☐	☐
read books for pleasure?	☐	☐	☐

HEALTH HABITS **Do you ...**	NEVER	SOMETIMES	OFTEN
bite your nails?	☐	☐	☐
smoke?	☐	☐	☐
exercise or play a sport?	☐	☐	☐
drink a lot of alcohol?	☐	☐	☐
eat junk food from fast food restaurants?	☐	☐	☐
drink coffee?	☐	☐	☐
drive too fast?	☐	☐	☐
get enough sleep?	☐	☐	☐

WRITING

Write two paragraphs.

1. In the first paragraph, write ten sentences about your good and bad habits. Mention things you do and don't do.
2. In the second paragraph, write ten sentences about your partner's habits. Describe things your partner does and doesn't do.

GRAMMAR TIP

Simple Present Negative Form

In the present tense, when the main verb is *be*, add *not* to form the negative. For all other verbs, add *do* or *does* and *not* before the base form of the verb.

Be: I **am** not rebellious. She **is** not lazy.

All other verbs: I **do** not **use** drugs. She **does** not **lie**.

To learn more about the simple present, see Unit 2 in *Avenues 1: English Grammar*.

WRITING Reflections

Write a paragraph that describes what type of person you are, entitled "The Truth about [your name]." Write at least ten sentences. Include photos or drawings. Provide answers to the following questions:

- What kind of person are you? Are you sociable or solitary?
- Do you have many responsibilities? What are they?
- Do you arrive for appointments or events late, early, or on time?
- Are you an early bird or a night owl? At what time of the day do you feel most active?
- Describe your living environment. Are you neat or messy?
- What are your passions?
- What do you value the most in your life?

Exchange Sheets

After you write your text, exchange sheets with a partner. Write down the first ten sentences from your partner's sheet, but change *I* to *he* or *she*. Remember to add -s or -es to verbs when the subject is third-person singular.

WATCHING Home: Two Points of View

Watch two videos that give definitions of home. In the first video, made for Lonely Planet, William Mitchell gives his personal definition of home. In the second video, Mathieu Favreau describes his home.

Watch both videos and answer the following questions on a separate sheet of paper.

WRITTEN RESPONSE

1 Write five questions that you would like to ask William. Also write five questions for Mathieu.

2 Write a paragraph of about 75 to 100 words giving your own definition of home. What does home mean to you? Is it a particular place? What makes you feel at home?

READING 1.3

READING CHALLENGE

WHEN DOES ADULTHOOD BEGIN? Does it start at a certain age? Does it begin with certain responsibilities? Barbara Ray discusses the trouble with adulthood.

My eLab

You can prepare for your reading tests by trying the reading strategies on pages 132-136. You can also practise by visiting My eLab. Click on Reading Strategies to find a variety of exercises.

sowed your wild oats: led an exciting lifestyle; had a lot of sexual relationships

The Trouble with Adulthood

BY BARBARA RAY

1 What does it mean to be "adult" today? I'm intrigued by this question. Or more accurately, I'm intrigued that we're asking the question. When I was growing up in the late 1970s/early 1980s, "adult" meant you were done with your education and had settled into a job that paid the bills. You were married and you probably owned a small "starter" home because renting was for college kids. You had a child in the backseat on your way to the grocery store. You had **sowed your wild oats**, and you were on your own. Oh, and you were twenty-five.

2 The path to adulthood was short and direct. Today, if you tell young people that to be an adult, they must be living on their own, earning their own way, with a spouse and a kid and a house—you will get a look of disbelief. "I'll never be an adult then" is their reply. Many people, of course, didn't take this short and direct path. But, on average, that path was the norm: leave home, get an education or training, get a job, marry, buy a home, have kids—in that order: boom, boom, boom.

3 I didn't follow the norm exactly. I messed around a little longer than most of my friends. I dropped out of college the first time, had a string of dead-end jobs, moved in with my boyfriend, and moved to another city. My messing around with this order was a **harbinger** of things to come. For underneath that fast and orderly path to adulthood were the **roilings** of change.

harbinger: predictor

roilings: stirring up or beginnings

unravel: fall apart; be destroyed

4 Indeed, the straight-shot embrace of adulthood began to **unravel** as early as the 1980s. A first sign was the number of young adults living at home with their parents for longer. The share of eighteen- to twenty-four-year-olds living at home rose slowly since the 1960s, but it jumped suddenly in the early 1980s—from 48 percent in 1980 to 54 percent in 1984. It hasn't changed that much since then.

floundered: had problems and made mistakes

5 Much of this so-called "failure to launch" is because of the rising demand for education and the longer time it takes to get that education. But of course, aspirations are one thing and completing a degree is quite another. Many **floundered** in school—and still do—dropping out, getting a job, figuring out that the job is going nowhere, and returning to school again. All this takes time. In the interim, all those other steps of adulthood get pushed back. And voila, the quick and direct path to adulthood isn't so quick or direct anymore.

6 At the same time, our ideas about marriage and family changed dramatically, as did our ideas of how to raise kids, what kind of home we liked, what a "necessity" was (cellphone anyone?). In short, this perfect storm of changing ideas and realities also changed our idea of what adulthood is.

7 Today, adulthood is more subjective. It's more often a feeling, not a thing. One young woman said she realized she was adult when, on a visit home, her dad offered her a beer and they talked politics—grown-up things. Another said she felt adult when she paid her own gas bill. One young woman said her sense of

being an adult goes in cycles. "I didn't really feel like an adult when I got married. I was just myself. But moving into our own place, and really getting into that routine of what our life was—paying bills, paying rent, car payments—that's when I really started to feel like an adult. I felt that way for a few years and then I went backwards a little when I moved home. And then backwards again to being a student."

8 The tried-and-true way of doing things has changed, and a "new normal" has begun to emerge. And that's where we stand today with the need to ask, "What is adulthood?"

(658 words)

COMPREHENSION

1 In the past, what were three features of adulthood?

____

2 In the past, at what age were most people considered adults, according to the writer? ______________

3 In paragraph 2, what is the meaning of *path*?

a. foot b. transit system c. road

4 In paragraph 3, what is the meaning of string?

a. thin cord b. series or succession c. flexible material

5 Did the writer follow the traditional route to adulthood? Explain your answer.

____

____

6 Why did the idea of adulthood change? List at least three reasons.

____

____

____

____

WRITING

1 Describe yourself. Are you an adult? Why or why not?

2 Describe your family. Do you have siblings (brothers and sisters) or are you an only child? How does your family situation affect your level of maturity?

TAKE ACTION!

WRITING TOPICS

Write about one of the following topics. For information about paragraph structure, see Writing Workshop 1 on page 137.

1 Good and Bad Habits

Write two paragraphs on habits. Explain how you and others behave at home and college.

Home Life: Consider your routines at home. Who do you live with? Who does the cooking and cleaning? What are your good and bad habits? What are the good and bad habits of someone who lives with you?

College Life: Consider your habits and routines at college. What are your work and study habits? Do you do homework on time? Do you prepare for exams in advance? Also describe the study habits of a good friend.

2 Adulthood

What are the characteristics of an adult? Is adulthood a period of time? Is it a stage of life? Go to My eLab and read "Marty's Life." Then, in a ten-sentence paragraph, define *adult*. Explain why Marty is, or is not, an adult.

SPEAKING TOPICS

Prepare a presentation on one of the following topics.

1 A Special Place

Where do you go when you feel stressed and you just want to relax? Think about a place that is very important to you. It could be a part of your home such as your bedroom, basement, or backyard. It could be a public place such as a park, restaurant, coffee shop, library, or dance club. It could also be a place where you go on vacation.

- Explain why the place is important to you.
- Describe how the place looks. Use *there is* and *there are* in your sentences.
- Explain what you usually do when you are in that place.

2 Your Home

Imagine that someone from another country is coming to visit you. Make a two-minute video about your home. Describe the place where you live and your neighbourhood. Also present the people who live in your home. What are their main characteristics?

SPEAKING PRESENTATION TIPS

- **Practise your presentation and time yourself.** You should speak for about two minutes (or for a length determined by your teacher).
- **Use cue cards.** Do not read! Put about fifteen keywords on your cue cards.
- **Bring visual support**, such as a picture, photograph, object, video, or PowerPoint slides.
- **Classmates will ask you questions about your presentation.** You must also ask your classmates about their presentations. Review how to form questions before your presentation day.

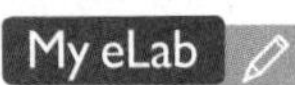

To practise vocabulary from this chapter, visit My eLab.

REVISING AND EDITING

REVISE FOR ADEQUATE SUPPORT

A good paragraph should include supporting ideas. Practise revising a student paragraph. First, read the paragraph. Then, add examples from your own life or the life of someone you know. Your examples will help make the paragraph more complete. (For more information about paragraph structure, see Writing Workshop 1 on pages 137-140.)

Our internal clock is the rhythm we have in our lives. It can determine when we wake up or go to bed. For example, I ______________________________

____

____

Our internal clock can also determine our eating schedule. Everyday, I ________

____

____

Finally, our internal clock can influence how punctual we are. My friend ________

____

____

EDIT PRONOUN USAGE

Practise editing a student paragraph. Underline and correct six pronoun errors, not including the example.

My friend Sylvain has some very bad habits. He lives with <u>her</u> (his) mother in Laval. He never helps she with the housework. When he finishes is meals, he doesn't wash the dishes. Sylvain he is spoiled because his mother cleans the house by himself. She doesn't ask his son to help. But Sylvain has some good qualities too. My friend he is a good driver. He respects the driving laws, and he drives safely.

GRAMMAR TIP

His or *Her*

Use *his* to show that a male possesses something.
Use *her* to show that a female possesses something.

Jonathan spoke to **his** mother. Isabel drives **her** son to daycare.

To learn more about pronouns, see Unit 1 in *Avenues 1: English Grammar.*

CHAPTER 2

HEALTH AND HAPPINESS

"The secret of happiness is to make others believe they are the cause of it."

— AL BATT

What makes you laugh? What do you do to feel better about yourself? In this chapter, you will read about strategies to develop a more positive outlook.

START UP Health and Lifestyle

Everyday Activities

Work with a small group. Take turns chatting about the following topics. You can change topics at any time. When the teacher flicks the lights on and off, change speakers.

1. My eating habits
2. My exercise habits
3. My sleep habits
4. My favourite activities

Using Question Words

Write the correct question word under each image. Choose words from the list below.

who	when	why	how far	how many
what	where	how often	how long	which

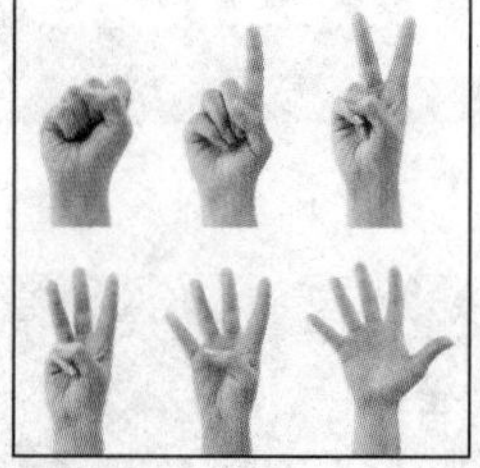

1 ____________

2 ____________

3 ____________

4 ____________

5 ____________

Frequency:
- ☐ once
- ☐ twice
- ☐ daily
- ☐ weekly

6 ____________

7 ____________

8 ____________

9 ____________

10 ____________

Health-Related Questions

On a separate piece of paper, write eight questions about health and lifestyle. Use the present tense. Try to use a variety of question words. Then ask a partner your questions and write down his or her answers. Your questions could be on the topics listed on page 21, or you can use your own ideas.

sleep	stress	food	dentist
work	exercise	relaxation	doctor

Example: **Question:** How often do you exercise every week?
Answer: Twice a week

WRITING

Write a paragraph about your partner. Include information from the health-related question activity.

GRAMMAR **TIP**

Forming Questions

Ensure that your questions have the proper word order.

Question word	auxiliary	subject	verb	rest of sentence.
How often	do	you	visit	the doctor?

To learn more about question forms, see the verb tense units in *Avenues 1: English Grammar*.

VOCABULARY **BOOST**

My eLab

You will also find this exercise in My eLab.

Internal Body Parts

Write the correct word next to each body part. Choose from the words in the box.

bladder	heart	kidneys	liver
brain	intestines	larynx	lungs

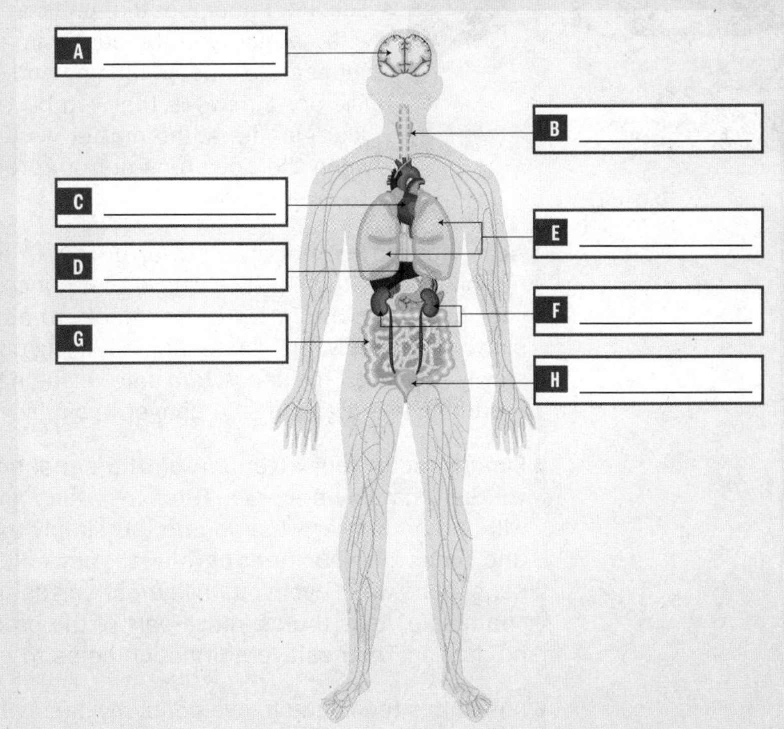

READING 2.1

ROHAN HEALY IS AN IRISH SINGER AND GUITARIST. Like about one in three adults, Rohan's response to stress was to have a panic attack. In the following essay, Healy explains how he stopped having panic attacks.

My eLab

You can prepare for your reading tests by trying the reading strategies on pages 132-136. You can also practise by visiting My eLab. Click on Reading Strategies to find a variety of exercises.

My Panic Attacks

BY ROHAN HEALY

1 At the age of nineteen, my life was difficult. There was illness in the family, I was unemployed, and I had very little money. This immense stress manifested in a series of panic attacks. Sometimes the panic attacks would occur outdoors. In crowded streets or cafés, I would hyperventilate, sweat, turn pale, and feel sick for no apparent reason. Sometimes my attacks would come in the night. My heart would beat rapidly as though I were running the 100-metre sprint. I would fear that I was going to die. I found some help through the books of celebrated panic expert Dr. Claire Weekes. There are certain steps you can take to combat panic attacks.

flight: the action of fleeing; running away

2 First, understand that a panic attack is a relatively harmless engagement of the body's survival response. When you feel stressed or anxious, you can inadvertently trigger the "fight or **flight**" response. This response fools the brain and nervous system into thinking there is an actual physical threat that requires you to defend yourself or run away. Your heart palpitates and provides more oxygen for your muscles, which are ready for action. You then worry about the mysterious behaviour of your body: "Why is my heart racing? Why am I sweating? Why is it difficult to breathe?" Of course, if you are being chased or if a car almost hits you, then you have a context and can understand the physical symptoms. But when you are lying in bed at night and the survival response is triggered, it's terrifying. Remember that panic attacks are not dangerous and they will not kill you.

3 Second, remember that panic attacks are time-limited. When faced with danger, your bloodstream is pumped with adrenaline, which causes the most confusing and scary symptoms of a panic attack. The good news is that you have a limited supply of adrenaline in your glands, so no matter what you do, the panic attack will end when the body runs out of adrenaline, after about thirty minutes. You will not die.

4 Next, deep breathing is a powerful tool in overcoming and shortening panic attacks. Unlike the heart, which you cannot control, you can consciously override your breath. In the midst of an attack, or as you feel one coming on, breathe slowly and deeply into your abdomen, filling up your whole belly and chest before slowly exhaling. This sends "I'm safe" signals to the brain because deep, relaxed breathing is a sign that the danger has passed.

5 Finally, focus your attention on the sensations in your body while reminding yourself that you are safe. The sensations are not physically harmful, and they will end no matter what you do, so simply experience them. Feel the tingling, and focus on your beating heart, your cold face, and the shaking. Let the sensations wash over you while breathing deeply and staying present. Repeating "I am safe" tells the cognitive part of the brain that all is well and that there is no danger. The positive affirmation helps to end the attack sooner.

6 I used this technique to overcome my panic attacks, and now they are very rare. If I ever feel one coming, I am able to quell the fight/flight/flee response quickly. So remember that panic attacks can do you no physical harm. Even if it feels

like your heart is beating out of your chest, it's not even beating as hard as it would if you were, say, running to catch a bus or playing a game of soccer. Remember that there's nothing physically wrong with you, and it's a natural response to fear and danger. Although it takes a little time and courage, you can overcome panic attacks just like I did.

(621 words)

COMPREHENSION

ESSAY STRUCTURE

1 This essay contains a thesis statement. The thesis statement is a sentence that sums up the main idea of the essay. Highlight the thesis statement.

2 Each body paragraph has a topic sentence. The topic sentence sums up the main idea of that paragraph. Underline the topic sentences in paragraphs 2 to 5.

Note: For more information about thesis statements and topic sentences, see pages 138-139 in Writing Workshop 1.

GENERAL UNDERSTANDING

3 What is the body's survival response? See paragraph 2. ______________________

____

4 When did Rohan experience his first panic attack? ______________________

____

5 Why do panic attacks feel so scary? ______________________

____

____

Circle *T* for "true" or *F* for "false." Write a true sentence under any false statements.

6 A panic attack can occur at any time, day or night. **T** **F**

____

7 A panic attack can last for many hours. **T** **F**

____

8 The body has a limited amount of adrenaline. **T** **F**

____

9 Panic attacks are dangerous, and the heart can stop beating. **T** **F**

____

10 Rohan no longer has panic attacks. **T** **F**

____

My eLab

Answer additional reading and listening questions in My eLab. You can also access audio and video clips online.

DISCUSSION

Do you have panic attacks? What are some positive ways to deal with stress?

SPEAKING Strong Emotions

Work with a partner. Write the correct word under each image. Use each word only once. You can use a dictionary if necessary.

afraid	annoyed	bored	deceived
depressed	disgusted	proud	thrilled

1 Kelly is ________________. The meeting is really long.

2 Maria just won $10,000. She is ________________!

3 Marcus feels a little angry. He is ________________ with his girlfriend because she is late.

4 They are ________________ of their son Kyle because he graduated from university.

5 Jeremy is feeling blue. He is ________________ because his partner broke up with him.

6 Melanie is ________________ because someone is following her.

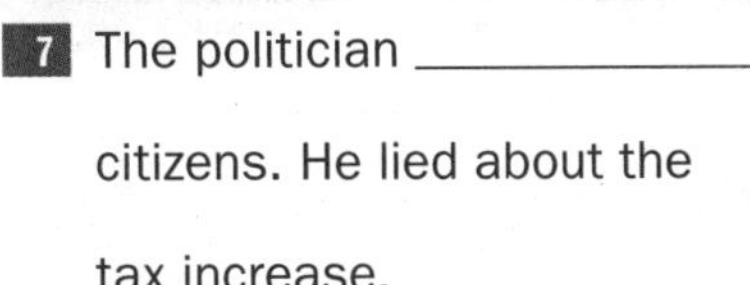

7 The politician ________________ citizens. He lied about the tax increase.

8 Alexa is ________________ because she sees a spider in her drink.

My eLab

Visit My eLab to practise using vocabulary related to emotions.

WRITING

In a paragraph, describe a time in the past when you felt one of the emotions listed in the previous activity. Explain what happened.

WATCHING 2.1 Living in Denmark

When you imagine the happiest place on Earth, you might pick a spot with warm sand and soft breezes—a Mediterranean village, perhaps. Learn about the happiest place on Earth. Watch the video and answer the questions.

COMPREHENSION

1 Which country ranked much higher on the "happiness" scale?

a. Iceland b. Fiji

2 What is the main complaint of most people in Denmark?

____

3 In Denmark, what is the concept of *yentala*?

a. Everyone must pay taxes.

b. Happiness is life's most important goal.

c. One person is not better than another—people are equal no matter what job they do.

4 What does Jan do for a living? ________________________________

5 Why does Jan do that job? ________________________________

____

6 What is unusual about Josef? ______________________________

____

7 Describe the Danish concept of *hooga*. ______________________________

____

8 Why are people in Denmark so happy? List at least three reasons.

____

____

____

DISCUSSION / WRITING

Is your country a great place to live? Why or why not? What are the advantages and disadvantages of living in your country?

READING 2.2 WITH LISTENING

WHAT FACTORS CONTRIBUTE TO RESILIENT BEHAVIOUR? A university professor decided to find out.

PRE-READING ACTIVITY

Answer the following questions. Then read the essay, "Developing Resilience."

1 When you get a low mark on a test, what do you tell yourself to justify it?

a. I deserved it. I am a poor student and I can't do well in college.
b. I probably didn't study enough. I'll do better next time.
c. The test was too hard. It was not fair.

2 When you woke up this morning, what were some of your thoughts?

a. How many days are left until the weekend?
b. I have too many things to do.
c. Here is another day. I'm going to enjoy it.

My eLab

You can prepare for your reading tests by trying the reading strategies on pages 132-136. You can also practise by visiting My eLab. Click on Reading Strategies to find a variety of exercises.

3 Look at the cartoon panel. Write what you think is going through the player's head. Write the first idea that comes to you.

GRAMMAR LINK

As you read, you will see some verb choices in parentheses. Highlight or underline the correct word. In My eLab, you can listen to this essay and check your answers. While you are listening, pay attention to the speaker's intonation and pronunciation.

Developing Resilience

collapse: fall apart; break down

1 Why (do / does) some people **collapse** under life stresses? Why do others survive traumatic circumstances such as severe illness, the death of loved ones, poverty, abuse, or war? Psychologists (know / knows) that there is no single source of resilience. Many factors come into play, including genetic predispositions, social skills, and self-esteem. But one character trait, above all others, (seem / seems) to help people cope, and that is the ability to maintain an optimistic attitude. Optimistic thinking can alleviate depression, and it has clear physical health benefits.

2 There (is / are) many examples of individuals who overcame tragic pasts. Both Maya Angelou and Oprah Winfrey were sexually abused and raised in poverty, yet Maya became a successful author and Oprah became one of the wealthiest talk show hosts in America. Holocaust survivor Gerda Weissmann Klein watched as soldiers took her parents away in June, 1942. Later, the Nazis captured her brother. Klein spent the rest of World War II in a concentration camp. In spite of the horrors that she witnessed, Klein and her husband say that their conversations are of hope and their language of optimism.

land mine: explosive device hidden underground

3 Jerry White is the author of *I Will Not Be Broken: Five Steps to Overcoming a Life Crisis*. When he was twenty years old, he took a backpacking trip through northern Israel with some friends. While walking up a hill, White stepped on a **land mine**. It exploded, and White lost a portion of his leg. He wrote, "You must choose a new path out of your personal nightmare. Passivity is a killer. Choosing life (require / requires) a willingness to fight."

4 Some researchers (say / says) that a positive outlook is more important than a realistic one. Optimists look at problems as a challenge. They do not focus on the past. They avoid self-recrimination and guilt. Instead, they face the facts. They focus on possible outcomes, and then move forward. They choose to believe that their lives have a purpose.

5 Because optimistic thinking (have / has) mental and physical health benefits, some researchers are training people to become optimists. Psychologist Andrew Shatte is the co-director of the Resiliency Project at the University of Pennsylvania. Shatte and a team of graduate students are teaching resilience to children. The key, Shatte says, is fighting depression.

self-defeating: not helpful; expecting to fail

6 In a pilot program, Shatte's psychology students showed seventy children how to develop more optimistic thinking patterns. For twelve weeks, the children learned that there is a strong connection between how they think and how they feel. They also learned to tell the difference between **self-defeating** thinking and productive thinking. Children looked at their own fears and asked, "What (is / are) the worst thing that could happen?" They had to test their expectations and see if they were realistic. They also learned problem-solving skills.

7 According to Andrew Shatte, children (learn / learns) optimistic thinking when they face challenges. For example, a researcher showed a cartoon to students. In the cartoon, a coach is pointing at a zero score and angrily looking at the players. Students had to write what the player is thinking. One child wrote, "We let the coach down. We're the worst team ever." Another wrote, "He's so mean! It's making me sad." But ten-year-old Bryce Marcus exhibited positive thinking. He wrote, "The coach can be mad. So what? We'll do better next time." The three students had different internal dialogues, which led to different emotional reactions.

8 A child who came from a dangerous inner-city neighbourhood was helped by the Penn Resiliency Program. Miguel believed that he would end up in a gang. He told the group, "What is the point in doing anything? It is just the way it is." In the program, Miguel had to "de-catastrophize" the situation. He changed his thinking and looked for other possible outcomes. The boy learned that he (don't / doesn't) have to focus on the worst-case scenarios. He can focus his energy on things that he can control. He can change the way he thinks, and he can choose solutions.

9 According to Jerry White, "They say what doesn't kill you makes you stronger. It's not quite that simple. I believe you have to decide it will make you stronger." There (is / are) ways to reframe how people perceive life's setbacks. "Life is too short and too beautiful for us to remain victims," White says.

(704 words)

Sources:
Andrews, Valerie. "Can You Teach Resilience?" *WebMD Medial News*. WordPress, 22 Oct. 2010. Web.
Aubrey, Allison. "Resilience Helps Kids Fight Depression." *Morning Edition*. National Public Radio. 19 Jan. 2010. Radio.
"Gerda Weissmann Klein." *Personal Histories*. United States Holocaust Memorial Museum, n.d. Web.
White, Jerry. *I Will Not Be Broken: Five Steps to Overcoming a Life Crisis*. New York: St. Martin's Griffin, 2009. Print.

COMPREHENSION

GENERAL UNDERSTANDING

1 What does *alleviate* mean? Find the word in paragraph 1 and make a guess. (Circle the letter of the correct answer.)

a. increase; grow larger　　b. reduce; diminish　　c. happiness

2 What do Oprah Winfrey, Maya Angelou, and Gerda Weissmann Klein have in common?

a. They are all Holocaust survivors.

b. They are all on television.

c. They all survived traumatic events in the past.

3 In paragraph 3, what point does Jerry White make?

a. People become stronger after a difficult event.

b. People can make a conscious choice to try to be stronger after a difficult event.

c. Life is not simple, and bad things do not make you stronger.

4 What is Andrew Shatte's job?

a. teacher　　b. student　　c. psychologist　　d. writer

MAIN IDEA

5 What is the main idea of paragraph 8?

a. Miguel, a child from a poor neighbourhood, learned to change the way he thinks about his life.

b. Miguel is from a dangerous neighbourhood.

c. People should be positive.

6 What is the main idea of this reading?

a. Andrew Shatte is a teacher of resilience.

b. Some people are optimists and others are pessimists.

c. People can become more resilient when they learn positive-thinking techniques.

d. Everybody is really an optimist.

WRITING

Think about a difficult moment in your past. What happened? How did you react? Write a paragraph about your experience.

Pleasure

Work with a partner. Ask your partner the following questions. Write your partner's answers in the spaces provided. You can write words or sentences.

Partner's name: ________________________

1 A comedy is a funny movie. In your opinion, what are two of the best comedies?

____

____

2 Who are your favourite comedians? (A comedian is a performer who tells jokes or performs acts to make people laugh.)

____

3 Think about the world's funniest movie. What is the movie about? In two or three sentences, describe the story.

____

____

____

4 Who is your best friend? ________________________

What do you appreciate about this friend? ________________________

____

____

5 Which activities do you love to do? Number your top five in order of preference.

_____ spend time outdoors in nature (walking, taking photos, and so on)

_____ have a hot bath

_____ do an exciting sport (skiing, snowboarding, skateboarding, cycling)

_____ go to a club or restaurant with friends

_____ go online to search social media sites, play games, and browse

_____ stay home with your favorite person

_____ play with your pet (dog, cat, horse, etc.)

_____ spend time alone with a warm drink and a good book

_____ (other)

6 What is your favourite way to spend a few hours? _______________

____

____

WRITING

Write a paragraph about your partner. In your paragraph, include your partner's answers from the speaking activity. Remember to begin your paragraph with a topic sentence. (For more information about topic sentences, see pages 138-139 in Writing Workshop 1.)

VOCABULARY BOOST

Humour

Fun means "pleasant" or "a pleasant time."

Funny means "humorous."

Humour (n.) means "the quality of being funny."

My trip to the beach was **fun**. We had a **fun** day. Kayan is so **funny**. He makes me laugh. He has a great sense of **humour**.

PRACTICE

Fill in the blanks with the correct words. Choose *fun*, *funny*, or *humour*.

Jeremy is a really joyful guy. Every day, he has a lot of __________. Often, he tells __________ jokes.

He has a great sense of __________. He could be a stand-up comedian! He is so __________ that we roll on the floor laughing. When we spend time with him, we always have __________.

READING 2.3

READING CHALLENGE

EVERYONE IS SEARCHING FOR HAPPINESS. But is it realistic to think we can be happy all of the time? The following essay looks at the truth about happiness. As you read, you will see expressions in bold. Try to guess what the expressions mean.

My eLab

You can prepare for your reading tests by trying the reading strategies on pages 132-136. You can also practise by visiting My eLab. Click on Reading Strategies to find a variety of exercises.

The Truth about Happiness

BY FRANK T. McANDREW

1 We often hear people start a sentence by saying, "It will be great when ..." We probably say this most frequently when we are young: It will be great when I get my driver's licence. It will be great when I go off to college and get out of my parents' house. It will be great when I get out of college and get a real job. It will be great when I fall in love and get married. Similarly, mostly older people start sentences with the phrase, "Wasn't it great when ...?" Think about how seldom you hear, "Isn't this great, right now?" Surely, our past and future moments are not always superior to our present ones, and yet we persist in thinking that this is the case. These **hiccups** in our thinking are mild delusions that are probably a very adaptive part of the human psyche.

hiccups: repetitions

2 Most of us have an *optimistic bias* about our future. As a classroom demonstration of this, at the beginning of a new term, I often ask students in my class to tell me—anonymously in a survey—what their grade point average (GPA) was last term and also ask them to estimate what it will be this term. I then give them accurate information about the average grade received by all students in this very class over the past three years and ask them to report the grade that they expect to receive. The demonstration **works like a charm** every time. Without fail, the predicted grades are far higher than one would reasonably expect given the evidence at hand. And yet, we believe.

3 Cognitive psychologists have also identified a phenomenon that they refer to as the *Pollyanna principle*. **In a nutshell**, it means that we process, rehearse, and remember pleasant information from the past more than unpleasant information from the past. An exception to this pattern would be depressed individuals who continually ruminate upon past failures and disappointments. Thus, for most of us, the reason that the good old days seem so good is that we focus on the pleasant stuff and tend to forget the day-to-day unpleasant stuff.

striving: working toward a goal

4 These innocent forms of self-deception enable us to keep **striving**. If our past was good and our future can be even better, then we can work our way out of the unpleasant, or at least mundane, present. Individuals in our evolutionary past who were not so delusional would have been out-competed by the **cock-eyed** optimists big time, and it is these "cock-eyed" genes that have come down through the ages to us.

cock-eyed: foolish; absurd

fleeting: transitory; passing quickly

5 All of this tells us something about the **fleeting** nature of happiness. Emotion researchers know about something called the "hedonic treadmill effect." We work very hard to reach a goal, anticipating the happiness that it will bring. After a brief fix of "yippee," we quickly slide back to our baseline, sorry-ass, mundane way of being and start **chasing the next carrot at the end of the stick**. Studies of lottery winners and individuals at the top of their fields who seem to "have it all" regularly **throw cold water on** our dreams that getting what we really want will change our lives. Assistant professors who dream of attaining tenure, and

lawyers who dream of becoming partners, often quickly find themselves wondering why they were in such a hurry. After finally publishing a book, it was depressing for me to realize how quickly my self-concept went from "I am a guy who wrote a book" to "I am a guy who has only written one book." Time to get back in the race.

seek: look for
bliss: happiness

6 This is all as it should be, at least from a competition point of view. Dissatisfaction with the present and dreams of the future are what keep us motivated, and warm fuzzy memories of the past reassure us that the feelings we **seek** can be had. Perpetual **bliss** would completely undermine our will to do anything at all, and people who remained happy for too long would get left behind. This should not be depressing to us; quite the contrary. Recognizing that happiness exists to keep us moving and that it is a delightful **visitor that never overstays its welcome** may help us appreciate it more when it arrives. It may also be useful to remind ourselves that there is nothing wrong with us if we think that our present life could be a lot better than it is—it is the human condition.

(757 words)

Source:
McAndrew, Frank T. "You Can't Be Happy All of the Time But Don't Stop Trying." *Psychology Today.* Sussex Publishers, 1 Mar. 2002. Web. 6 Aug. 2015.

COMPREHENSION

IDIOMATIC EXPRESSIONS

1 The following expressions are idioms. They have meanings that do not necessarily match the meaning of the individual words. Write the letter of the best definition in the space provided. Remember to look at each expression in context. (The paragraph number is in parentheses.)

Terms		Definitions
1. work like a charm (2)	____	a. try to reach something that is not attainable
2. in a nutshell (3)	____	b. something that does not stay, or last, too long
3. chase the carrot at the end of the stick (5)	____	c. function consistently and easily
4. throw cold water on (5)	____	d. briefly; in short
5. visitor that never overstays its welcome (6)	____	e. discourage by being negative

MAIN IDEAS

2 Which sentence expresses the main—or principal—idea of paragraph 2?

a. Most people have an optimistic bias, or feeling, about the future.

b. The writer gives a test to her students each term.

c. Students make guesses about their grades.

d. Students always predict that their grades will be higher than the average.

3 What is not an example of the Pollyanna principle? Make a guess based on the information in paragraph 3.

a. I loved my kindergarten teacher.

b. My father was horrible and mean to me when I was a child.

c. My friend visited last weekend, and we had a fantastic time.

d. The meal last night was so tasty. Everything was good.

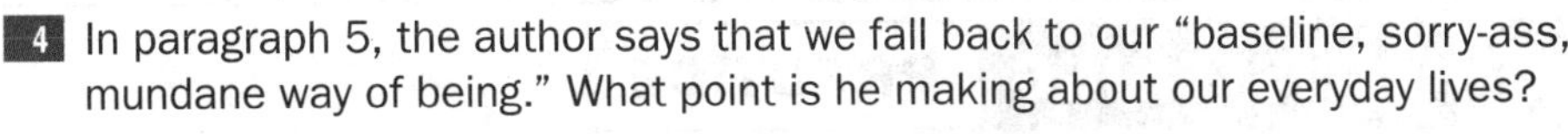

4 In paragraph 5, the author says that we fall back to our "baseline, sorry-ass, mundane way of being." What point is he making about our everyday lives?

____

____

5 What is the main idea of paragraph 5?

a. Happiness is something we can easily find.

b. Emotion researchers study the hedonic treadmill effect.

c. Happy moments pass quickly; they don't last long.

d. After the author wrote a book, he wondered when he would write another book.

6 According to the writer, why is it good that we can't always be happy?

____

____

SPEAKING Daily Happiness Exercises

Happiness researchers, such as psychologist Shawn Achor, developed some ways to transform pessimists into optimists. Here are some of his happiness exercises.

1 **Meditation:** Take two minutes to concentrate on your breathing.

2 **Gratitude:** Write down at least three things you are grateful for. They don't have to be profound. You can write about simple things, such as looking at a flower or drinking a good cup of coffee.

3 **Best experience:** Choose one experience from your day, and spend two minutes writing about that experience.

4 **Exercise:** Do fifteen minutes of a cardio activity that you really enjoy, such as walking the dog.

5 **Act of kindness:** Each day, do one act that will make someone feel better. Compliment your mom, or send a text message to a friend with words of praise, or smile at a stranger. When you make others feel good, you will feel better too.

6 **Social connections:** Spend some time every day having a conversation with a family member or friend. Look that person in the eye and listen. Social connections can help you feel better.

Source: "Shawn Achor's Six Exercises for Happiness." *CBC News*. CBC/Radio-Canada, 22 Apr. 2015. Web.

WRITING

Try doing as many of these activities as you can for one week. Keep a journal. Record your feelings of gratitude and describe your best experiences.

LISTENING PRACTICE

1. Pronounce *–s* Verb Endings

When present tense verbs follow a third-person singular subject, the verb ends in *–s* or *–es*. There are different ways to pronounce the final ending.

PRONUNCIATION TIP

Third-person Singular

Most verbs end in an *–s* or a *–z* sound.

Examples: write - writes [s] love - loves [z]

Add *–es* to verbs ending in *–s*, *–ch*, *–sh*, *–x*, or *–z*. Pronounce the final *–es* as a separate syllable.

Examples: push - pushes [pushiz] reach - reaches [reachiz]

Pronounce each verb after the speaker. You will say each verb twice. Then indicate if the verb ends with an *–s*, a *–z*, or an *–iz* sound. Circle the correct choice.

1	hopes	s	z	iz	6	forces	s	z	iz
2	races	s	z	iz	7	feels	s	z	iz
3	watches	s	z	iz	8	teaches	s	z	iz
4	laughs	s	z	iz	9	kisses	s	z	iz
5	tries	s	z	iz	10	smiles	s	z	iz

2. Pronounce Sentences in the Simple Present

Repeat each sentence after the speaker. Then fill in the blanks with the words that you hear. You can use contracted forms.

Example: Samuel ____talks____ on his cellphone every day.

1 Emily ________________ to watch videos online.

2 She ________________ her television.

3 Many people ________________ for DVDs.

4 Emily downloads movies and ________________ them.

5 Samuel ________________ his cellphone constantly.

6 Every day, he ________________ his phone in his pocket.

7 Samuel ________________ a landline telephone.

8 He ________________ long-distance calls.

9 They ________________ addictions to technology.

10 Emily ________________ how to live without a computer.

WATCHING 2.2 Meditation and Its Effects on the Brain

What are the effects of meditation on the brain? To find out, watch this report from *ABC News*. Begin by listening to the first part of the report and completing the vocabulary exercise. Then listen to the rest of the report and answer the comprehension questions.

VOCABULARY

Listen carefully to the beginning of the video and fill in the missing words.

1 It's intimate, and intense. It can be done ______________ or with others. And ______________ million Americans are trying it, including shock jock Howard Stern, actors Richard Gere, Goldie Hawn and Heather Graham, and the lead ______________ of the rock band Weezer. What do these people ______________ about that we don't? Meditation.

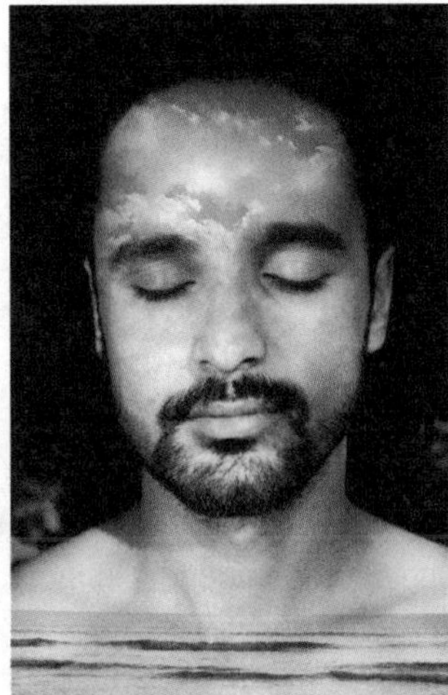

COMPREHENSION

2 Some regular people took a meditation course. How long did the course last?

a. two days b. six weeks c. eight weeks d. six months

3 Which parts of the participants' brains grew after they meditated?

a. the local brain
b. the parts associated with compassion
c. the parts associated with stress

4 What are some of the effects of taking the meditation course? Give two or three examples of changes in people's behaviour.

____

____

____

5 What are the steps to meditating?

Step 1: ______________________________________

Step 2: ______________________________________

Step 3: ______________________________________

6 Which sentence is true about the Dalai Lama?

a. The Dalai Lama never becomes angry.
b. The Dalai Lama laughs a lot.
c. The Dalai Lama is enlightened.

TAKE ACTION!

WRITING TOPICS

Write about one of the following topics. For information about paragraph and essay structure, see the Writing Workshops (pages 137-147).

1 Pleasure

Write two paragraphs. In your first paragraph, describe what you do for fun. Who do you do that activity with?

For your second paragraph, choose a photograph that captures a pleasurable moment from your past. Provide a copy of that photo and describe what was happening when the picture was taken.

2 Health Habits

Write about your health habits. Also describe the health habits of a friend or family member. Discuss one or more of the following topics:

exercise eating relaxation sleep

3 Resilience

Look again at the essay, "Developing Resilience." Then write about yourself. In the first paragraph, discuss your attitude to life. Are you a positive or negative person? How do you deal with stressful situations in life?

In your second paragraph, describe a difficult situation you went through in the past. What happened? How did you deal with the situation?

SPEAKING TOPICS

Prepare a presentation about one of the following topics.

1 Gratitude Video

Create a video or PowerPoint presentation about things in life that you are grateful for. To plan for your presentation, create a gratitude journal. Consider what you feel is most worthwhile. Explain why each person, event, or item is important to you.

2 Commercial about Health

Make an audio or video commercial aimed at college and university students. Convince students to take care of their health. For example, warn students about the dangers of certain drugs, or encourage them to exercise. Use your imagination.

My eLab

Visit My eLab to practise vocabulary from this chapter.

SPEAKING PRESENTATION TIPS

- **Practise your presentation and time yourself.** You should speak for about two minutes (or for a length determined by your teacher).
- **Use cue cards.** Do not read! Put about fifteen keywords on your cue cards.
- **Bring visual support,** such as a picture, photograph, object, video, or PowerPoint slides.
- **Classmates will ask you questions about your presentation.** You must also ask your classmates about their presentations. Review how to form questions before your presentation day.

REVISING AND EDITING

REVISE FOR A MAIN IDEA

The following paragraph contains supporting details, but it has no main idea. A main idea is expressed in a topic sentence. Read the paragraph, and add a good topic sentence. (For more information about topic sentences, see Writing Workshop 1, pages 137-140).

Topic sentence: ____

____

First, exercise slows brain deterioration in patients who have Alzheimer's disease. According to the Canadian Broadcasting Corporation (CBC), "exercise actually slows down age-related brain cell death." Furthermore, exercise promotes brain cell growth. Finally, exercise helps the brain learn. In a Saskatoon school for at risk students, gym equipment was put in a classroom. Before doing math, students had to work out on a treadmill for half an hour. The teacher discovered that the students had better results after they exercised. Thus, the link between exercise and the brain is becoming clear.

EDIT PRESENT TENSE VERBS

Practise editing a student paragraph. Underline and correct five errors with simple present tense verbs, not including the example.

My parents have very different personalities. My stepfather make a lot of jokes. He works in a bank, and he don't like his job. However, when he is home, he laugh a lot. My mother, on the other hand, is the disciplinarian. When she gets angry, she usually have a very good reason. For example, my younger brother is very rude, and he don't do his homework, so my mom often yells at him.

GRAMMAR TIP

Don't or Doesn't

Be careful when writing negative verb forms in the simple present tense. Remember that the apostrophe replaces the *o* in *not*.

I, you, we, or *they*	+ *don't*	+ base form of verb
He, she, it	+ *doesn't*	+ base form of verb

We **don't** eat junk food. She **doesn't** use Instagram.

To learn more about the simple present, see Unit 2 in *Avenues 1: English Grammar.*

CHAPTER 3

CONSUMER TRENDS

"Our personal consumer choices have ecological, social, and spiritual consequences."

— DAVID SUZUKI

Every year, there are new trends and fashions. Are you a slave to trends, or do you make your own style decisions? This chapter examines consumer trends.

START UP Trends

Possessions

Work with a small group. Take turns chatting about the following topics. You can change topics at any time. When the teacher flicks the lights on and off, change speakers.

1. My favourite pieces of clothing
2. My cellphone's good and bad features
3. My most valuable possession
4. Things I want to buy

What's the Trend?

A trend is an activity, fashion, or item that is very popular for a short period of time. Look at the three clues, and try to guess the name of the game or trend. Write the name in the space provided.

Clues				Game or Trend
	Example: trivia	questions	phone app	Trivia Crack
1	140 characters	tweet	short messages	______________
2	cube	colours	match the sides	______________
3	classic video game	warfare	Call ...	______________
4	flat	throw it	resembles a plate	______________
5	"Snap"	photo disappears	my story	______________
6	Supercell	clans	phone app	______________
7	men	hairstyle	bun	______________
8	friend me	status update	my wall	______________
9	phone app	dating	swipe left or right	______________
10	puzzle	numbers	Japanese	______________
11	classic video game	brothers	Luigi	______________
12	phone app	game	birds	______________
13	jumping	dangerous activity	wings	______________
14	skateboard	scooter	balance	______________
15	photo share	"instant"	square pictures	______________

READING 3.1

READ ABOUT THE VARIOUS TRICKS MARKETERS PLAY ON US. Write a short definition of each highlighted word on the line opposite. Use context clues to guess the meaning of the words. (To learn more about context clues, see pages 132-133.)

Write definitions.

Example: shoppers

Marketing New Trends

1 What brand of shoes are you wearing today? What type of phone do you have? What are your favourite apps? Every year, there are new trends. They could be a fashion such as a new shirt style, an activity such as scooter boarding, or an object such as a new phone. Advertisers are masters at convincing **consumers** to modify their spending habits and follow new trends.

2 **Great slogans:** Great advertising slogans can change the way people shop and spend money. For instance, Hallmark, established in 1910, originally created postcards. But when the company **shifted** into greeting cards, it influenced the way people celebrate. With the slogan, "When you care enough to give the very best," greeting cards became obligatory for most holidays. Mother's Day, Father's Day, Christmas, Valentine's Day, and birthdays are also known as "Hallmark Holidays."

3 A great slogan also influenced the way people celebrate love and marriage. The compulsory diamond engagement ring was an invention of a diamond company, De Beers. In 1947, the company **came up with** the slogan, "A diamond is forever." Advertisements equated a man's love with how much he was **willing** to spend on a ring. By the 1950s, diamond rings came to symbolize enduring love and marriage. Today, most grooms feel compelled to shop for a diamond ring, all because of a great advertising **gimmick**.

4 **Fear marketing:** Companies can take advantage of common fears to create new trends. For instance, in 1977, Perrier ads capitalized on the public's anxiety about pollution and the quality of tap water, and the bottled water fad was born. Suddenly, even though the nation's tap water generally met or exceeded safety standards, consumers became convinced that bottled water was better, and bottled water sales **soared**.

5 Another example is the fear of bird flu and other diseases, which helped soap companies create the "antibacterial" trend. The traditional bar of soap kills almost as many germs as antibacterial soap, but **clever** campaigns convinced consumers they needed the new—and often higher-priced—antibacterial product.

6 **Insecurity marketing:** Companies can also modify human behaviour simply by playing on people's insecurities. In 1912, high school student Edna Murphey created a company to sell her father's invention: an antiperspirant called Odorono (Odor? Oh no!). At first, she was not successful. People believed that perfume was adequate and that blocking sweat was unhealthy. Plus, the product could burn skin and **stain** clothing. In fact, one customer complained that Odorono destroyed her wedding dress. Sales stagnated until a smart copywriter, James Young, realized the power of marketing to take advantage of people's insecurities. A new campaign suggested that others would **gossip** about you if you had bad body odour. A *Ladies' Home Journal* ad showed a woman in a man's arms, with the caption "A woman may be stinky and offensive and not even know it!" The ad worked, and Odorono sales **skyrocketed**. Today, deodorant is an 18-billion-dollar industry.

7 **Appeals to emotion:** Most ads don't aim to reason with us. If they provided rational arguments for buying something, we would have to think about them. It would take effort. Instead, good ad campaigns target our emotions. The **pathway** to the emotional brain is quick and direct. So if an advertisement or slogan makes us feel good or scared or insecure, we will react instinctively. In the television series *Mad Men*, Don Draper says that advertisers sell happiness. "And do you know what happiness is? Happiness is the smell of a new car. It's freedom from fear. It's a **billboard** on the side of a road that screams 'You are OK.'"

8 Today, we are easier to influence than ever before. Online tracking can determine our age, gender, and preferences. Then marketing companies place targeted ads on our social media sites. So before you jump onto the next trend, remember that you are being manipulated by very smart advertisers.

(639 words)

Sources:
Everts, Sarah. "How Advertisers Convinced Americans They Smelled Bad." *Smithsonian*. Smithsonian.com, 2 Aug. 2012. Web.
Peretti, Jacques. "SUVs, Handwash and FOMO: How the Advertising Industry Embraced Fear." *The Guardian*. Guardian News and Media, 6 July 2014. Web.
Solomon, Michael R., Greg Marshall, and Elnora Stuart. *Marketing: Real People, Real Choices*. Upper Saddle River: Pearson, 2008. Print.

My eLab

You can prepare for your reading tests by trying the reading strategies on pages 132-136. You can also practise by visiting My eLab. Click on Reading Strategies to find a variety of exercises.

COMPREHENSION

MAIN AND SUPPORTING IDEAS

1 What is the main idea of the essay? ____________________

____

2 What is a slogan? ____________________

3 How did the following marketing techniques change consumer behaviour? Provide specific examples.

Slogans: Example: Hallmark convinced us we should give greeting cards for celebrations.

____

____

Fear marketing: ____________________

____

____

Insecurity marketing: ____________________

____

GRAMMAR LINK

4 Write the three questions that appear in paragraph 1.

____

____

____

My eLab

Answer additional reading and listening questions in My eLab. You can also access audio and video clips online.

5 Why does only one of the questions in paragraph 1 contain an *-ing* verb?

____

____

____

6 Why does only one of the questions in paragraph 1 contain the auxiliary *do*?

____

____

WATCHING 3.1 Fake Online Reviews

When you go to a restaurant or choose a movie, do you consult the online reviews? Watch this short ABC News clip about some unsavory practices.

COMPREHENSION

1 Many reviews are fake. What does *fake* mean? ______________

2 A fine is a sum of money imposed as a penalty. How many companies is the New York attorney general fining? ______________

3 How much money does Cassy Sailor receive for each online review that she posts? ______________

4 Cassy read a review aloud. What was the review about?

a. a restaurant

b. a car dealer

c. a bathroom renovation

d. a hair salon

5 How old is Cassy? ______________

6 Approximately what percentage of online reviews are fakes?

a. 10 percent b. 20 percent c. 30 percent d. 50 percent

7 Is it legal for companies to pay people to write fake reviews?

☐ Yes ☐ No

8 Why do companies post fake reviews? ______________

____

9 What does *caveat emptor* mean? ______________

DISCUSSION

With a partner or group, discuss the following questions:

- Which websites do you go to for reviews?
- Do online reviews influence you? Explain why or why not.

LISTENING PRACTICE

1. Identify Large Numbers

You will hear a speaker read out some numbers. Before you listen, review how to break down a large number.

Look at the number: 2,357,419,680

The number breaks down as follows:

2	Two billion
357	three hundred and fifty-seven million
419	four hundred and nineteen thousand
680	six hundred and eighty

The speaker will say sentences that include numbers. Circle the number you hear the speaker pronounce in each sentence. The speaker will repeat each sentence. (Notice that the dollar symbol appears before the number, not after.)

Example: Jerry earns ($40,000) / $4000 per year.

1. $15.95 / $50.95
2. 1982 / 1892
3. 6418 / 6480
4. $115.50 / $150.15
5. 1,000,000 / 1,000,000,000
6. 40 / 14
7. 2020 / 2002
8. $170,000 / $117,000
9. 13 / 30
10. $613,000 / $630,000

2. Pronounce Sentences

Repeat each sentence after the speaker. Then write the missing verb in the blank.

1. Consumer culture ________________ problems for the environment.
2. Ben ________________ a lot of money on his hobby.
3. He is a drummer, and drums ________________ expensive.
4. Right now, Ben ________________ drumsticks.
5. He ________________ with his credit card.
6. He rarely ________________ his credit card.
7. Chantal ________________ as a cashier.
8. Right now, she ________________ the money into the cash register.
9. At this moment, Chantal ________________ Ben his change.
10. The music store ________________ at 9 p.m.

LISTENING Generic Brands

If a product remains the number one brand for decades, it risks losing control of its trademark. Many pioneering brands suffered that fate. Just ask the makers of the board game Monopoly, who lost the right to their own trademark recently. Listen to this segment from *The Age of Persuasion*. Pay particular attention to the numbers that you hear.

COMPREHENSION

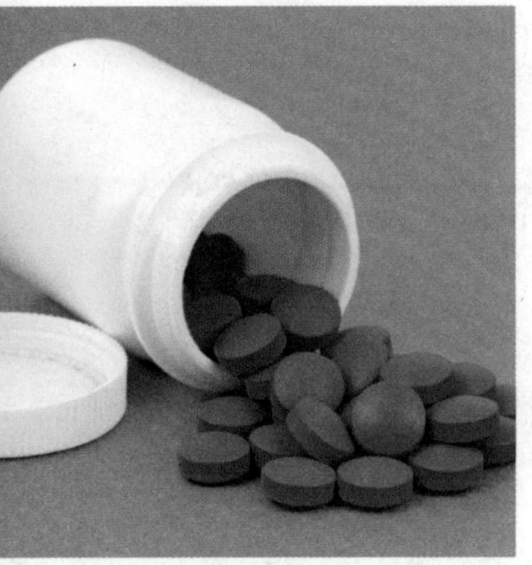

1. In what year was kitty litter invented? ______________
2. What did Kay Draper originally put in her cat's litter box?
   a. sand b. ashes c. both of the answers
3. How much did a bag of kitty litter originally sell for? ______________
4. Fifty years after he first started his company, Ed Lowe sold it. How much money did he receive? ______________
5. Why did Earl Dixon decide to create the first band-aid?
   a. His wife often cut and burned her fingers.
   b. He cut his finger on a machine at his workplace.
   c. He was an inventor and made many other products.
6. In what year was heroin discovered? ______________
7. Who discovered heroin? ______________
8. In 1899, Bayer exported heroin to how many countries? ______________
9. When was the *Harrison Narcotics Tax Act* passed? ______________
10. When the heroin trademark expired, what new product did Bayer launch? ______________

SPEAKING Name That Product

Work with a partner and come up with the names of five popular products or games. They can be products from the past or present. As you brainstorm ideas, think about games you played as a child, household gadgets, or fashion products.

Write down the titles of the products on small pieces of paper. Then join another pair of students. Those students must take turns guessing what your products are. They can only ask "yes/no" questions.

Example:	Is it circular?	Yes
	Does it have many parts?	No
	Does it go on your wrist?	Yes
	Does it count steps?	Yes
	(Answer: "FitBit bracelet")	

READING 3.2 WITH LISTENING

SOME PEOPLE TAKE SHOPPING TO AN EXTREME. Read about a compulsive shopper.

GRAMMAR LINK

As you read, you will see some word choices in parentheses. Underline or highlight the correct word. Note that *X* means "nothing." In My eLab, you can listen to this essay and check your answers. While you are listening, pay attention to the speaker's intonation and pronunciation.

The Compulsive Shopper

BY R. A. PARERA

1 While walking toward a clothing store, I think, "I do not need anything." I am aware that I have enough skirts, shoes, and purses, and I know that I should not waste my money. However, as I approach the entrance, my logic suddenly changes. "I will not buy anything ... unless it is too fabulous to leave behind." Finally, I enter the store, and all logic flies out the mannequin-adorned window. Inside the store, I feel happy and optimistic, like there isn't a care in the world besides finding the perfect top.

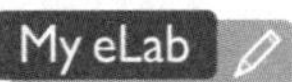

You can prepare for your reading tests by trying the reading strategies on pages 132-136. You can also practise by visiting My eLab. Click on Reading Strategies to find a variety of exercises.

2 Pretty much 70 percent of what I own I don't technically need. I can't even count the number of tops, pants, skirts, sweaters, or necklaces that I own. I have enough clothing to wear a completely different outfit every single (day / days) for two months.

3 Occasionally, I'll regret buying something. But I keep the tag on a piece of clothing until I wear it, so if I feel any regret, I'll return it. One recent item that I regretted buying was a full-body jumpsuit. It fit well but it puffed out at the hips and made me look like a fat genie. At the store, in my shopaholic haze, I thought, "I can pull this off. I can make this **wacky** outfit work." Well, once I was home and clear-minded, I realized just how very wrong I was. I returned it (a / the) next day, which might seem like a smart thing to do, except that instead of getting my money back, I exchanged it for two tops.

wacky: crazy

4 Although I have (a / an) shopping addiction, I am not wealthy. I graduated from college a year ago, and I work as a graphic designer. I earn just a bit over the minimum wage, and most of my salary goes toward my basic necessities. I no longer live at home, so I have to pay (for / X) food, rent, electricity, a bus pass, and so on. I am quite responsible. (This / These) days, I live on a budget and never go into debt. I do not squander large amounts of money on my shopping habit.

5 So, how do I manage to buy so (much / many) things? I find ways to fill my desperate craving but still keep money in the bank. I'm a bargain hunter, and there are many stores that sell very nice clothing for dirt cheap. Most of the stores I go into are very affordable. I love thrift (store / stores) and church basement sales, and I will buy second-hand clothing. At one church basement sale, I snagged a waist-length black leather jacket with silver buttons. It only cost $5, and it was the best bargain I ever found.

6 One of the (store / stores) that I visit has expensive clothes, but I walk straight to the sales section. I ignore everything else that I pass. I'm like a horse with blinders on. Once I'm among these inexpensive rows of clothing, and something catches my eye, I immediately look at the price and then apply the formula. If it costs as much as a meal, let's say $10 to $15, then I only need to wear it once to get my money's worth. If I'm willing to spend that money (in / on) food that

will only satisfy me for a couple of hours, why wouldn't I spend the same on a shirt? The more I think I would wear (a / an) item, the more I am willing to spend. And of course there is the "beautiful" exception. If something is absolutely to die for, I will spend up to $50 depending on how obsessed I am about the object.

7 I know that I shop too much, but I like the way I live. If it makes me appear to be a shallow consumer, I'm okay with that. I know in my heart that I am not superficial.

(654 words)

COMPREHENSION

VOCABULARY

On a separate piece of paper, use your own words to write definitions for the following terms. Use context clues. (The paragraph number is in parentheses.)

1. mannequin (1)
2. outfit (2)
3. tag (3)
4. cravings (5)
5. dirt cheap (5)
6. catch my eye (6)
7. to die for (6)
8. shallow (7)

WRITTEN RESPONSE

On a separate paper, write ten questions to ask the writer.

Example: Why do you shop so much?

VOCABULARY BOOST

Shopping Terms

For sale means "available to buyers."

My house is **for sale**.

On sale means "available at a reduced price."

Those pants are **on sale**. They're a bargain.

Sell (past form: sold) means "to offer something in exchange for money."

Sara **sells** shoes. She **sold** many shoes yesterday.

PRACTICE

Fill in the blanks with the correct words from the following list. Use each choice once only.

on sale   for sale   sell   sold

1. The Bechards are moving. There is a ____________ sign in front of their house.
2. If someone wants to ________ a second-hand item of clothing, Marcia might buy it. Last year, a man ________ a leather coat to Marcia for just $5. When Marcia shops, she searches for items that are ____________ because she hates to pay the full amount.

SPEAKING Fashion Trends

Describe what these people are doing. Also describe what they are wearing. Use complete sentences, and include colours and details in your descriptions. Try to use the following vocabulary in some of your sentences.

belt boots leather plaid striped skirt suit tie

He is wearing a leather jacket.

He is reading a book.

GRAMMAR TIP

Present Progressive

When an action is happening right now, use the present progressive tense. Form the present progressive with the appropriate form of *be* (*am*, *are*, *is*) and the *-ing* form of the verb. Add *not* to make negative sentences.

She **is wearing** boots. The woman **is not** standing.

To learn more about the present progressive tense, see Unit 3 in *Avenues 1: English Grammar.*

WATCHING 3.2 Damn Heels

On *Dragons' Den*, aspiring entrepreneurs pitch their business concepts and products to a panel of Canadian business moguls. Watch the episode and answer the questions.

COMPREHENSION

1 Describe the product called Damn Heels. ______________________

____

____

2 What is the name of the woman who invented the product?

a. Hailey Coleman b. Melanie Johnson c. Jane Smith

3 How many sizes do the ballet slippers come in? ______________

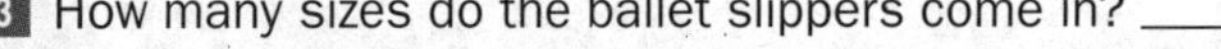

Kevin Jim Arlene Robert Brett

4 About how many units of Damn Heels has Hailey sold?

a. 200 b. 700 c. 3000

5 How much does one unit of Damn Heels cost? ________

6 Where are the main competitors to Damn Heels?

a. France b. United States c. the UK (United Kingdom)

7 What does Arlene offer?

a. $25,000 in cash and $25,000 in marketing expertise

b. $50,000 in cash

c. $50,000 in marketing expertise

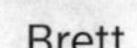

8 What royalty rate does Arlene want? ____________

9 What do the other Dragons think about Arlene's deal? ____________

____

WRITING

Go to cbc.ca or YouTube and watch another episode of *Dragons' Den*. Choose one of the ideas or products that you like. In a paragraph, describe it and explain why it is a good idea.

READING 3.3

THESE DAYS, MANY CONSUMERS ARE CHOOSING TO SHARE rather than to buy items. Read about the sharing economy.

My eLab

You can prepare for your reading tests by trying the reading strategies on pages 132-136. You can also practise by visiting My eLab. Click on Reading Strategies to find a variety of exercises.

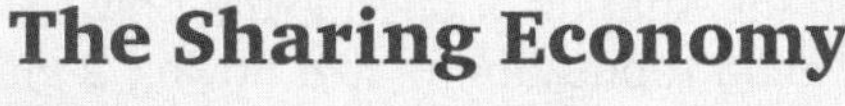

The Sharing Economy

BY TERRY O'REILLY

1 There is only one fate worse than death, and that is moving. The reason moving is so painful is because we suddenly rediscover all our stuff. Because we are a society of consumers, we are also a society of storage renters. In North America, storage facilities take up an area three times the size of Manhattan Island. There's an extraordinary amount of unused stuff sitting idle in storage facilities. But an interesting shift is **afoot**. It's a movement that resists ownership. People are happy to **borrow** when they need things. It's called the "sharing economy."

afoot: in progress
borrow: take something with the promise of returning it

2 The sharing economy has two main elements: the sharing of goods or the sharing of services. It is also called the peer-to-peer (P2P) market because it's a person-to-person transaction. Rachel Botsman, author of *What's Mine Is Yours*, explains it this way: "Sharing products without owning them is based primarily on products with a 'high-idling capacity.'" For example, there are over 80 million power drills in North American homes. The total time an average power drill will be used in its lifetime is just thirteen minutes. If you own a car, chances are it will sit in your driveway for twenty-three hours a day. That's the definition of "idling capacity"—many of the products in our lives simply sit idle and unused.

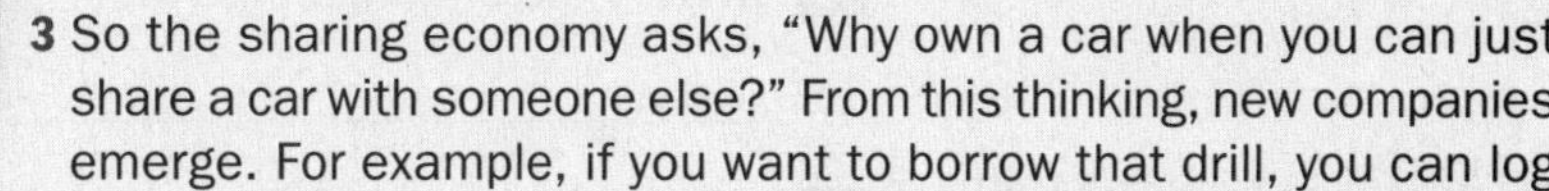

3 So the sharing economy asks, "Why own a car when you can just share a car with someone else?" From this thinking, new companies emerge. For example, if you want to borrow that drill, you can log onto Neighborgoods.net. It's a website that connects people with items to people who need items. In cities like Toronto or Halifax, you can borrow that drill from tool library websites.

4 Regarding cars, for decades you only had a few choices: buy, lease, or rent. Then along came companies like Zipcar. Suddenly, you could rent cars by the hour instead of by the day. Many people now have the option to rent a car for occasional errands, instead of owning a car that sits idle for most of the day. With Uber, you can use an app to hire private cabs. Uber is now in 53 countries and 250 cities. With those numbers, the big losers, of course, are **cab** and limo companies.

cab: taxi

5 If you want to rent out your own car that's sitting idle in your driveway—you can list your car with Relayrides.com in the States. The website will rent your car out for you and give you 75 percent of the rental charge, which is a bargain for renters because it is still cheaper than renting from an established rental company. That's great news for everybody—except Avis, Hertz, Budget, and the rest of the car rental companies.

6 One of the most successful sharing companies is Airbnb. One day, two design grads in San Francisco figured they could make a few extra bucks by offering airbeds in their loft to people who were attending a design conference. They set up a website called Air Bed and Breakfast.com—and made $1000 in one week. With that sudden success, the two grads decided to max out their credit cards and build a bigger site with more listings beyond their own apartment. They eventually changed the name to Airbnb—and last year, the site booked over 14 million nights around the world. Airbnb is eating into the business of low- and mid-priced hotels.

trumps: ranks above; is superior to

rate: judge and provide a value, such as a five-star rating

7 There are really two fundamental building blocks of the sharing economy: One is the belief that access **trumps** ownership. The other is trust among strangers. All sharing sites use reputations as currency. Borrowers **rate** lenders, lenders rate borrowers, and people can flag another member's account if something goes wrong. In the sharing economy, the only thing people want to own is their reputation. A good reputation is like having a giant key that will open multiple doors. Young people just don't want to own the door.

8 The sharing economy is bad news for brands because it is stealing market share from traditional corporations. Both UberX and Lyft are facing legal fights. Established cab companies are filing lawsuits claiming car-sharing companies don't adhere to rules and regulations. In many cities, the hotel industry is lobbying governments to stop Airbnb.

9 But the sharing economy also has an upside: it helps make the environment better. Less stuff is manufactured, fewer products are purchased, and there is less waste. Twentieth century laws are going to have to give way to twenty-first century realities, and big brands will have to figure out strategies to coexist with sharing sites.

(760 words)

Source:
O'Reilly, Terry. "The Sharing Economy." *Under the Influence*. CBC Radio-Canada, 21 July 2015. Radio.

COMPREHENSION

VOCABULARY

1 What is the sharing economy? ______________________

____

2 In paragraph 2, what does *idle* mean?

a. lazy and unproductive b. not being used c. cold

3 In paragraph 7, the author says, "people can flag another member's account if something goes wrong." What does *flag an account* mean?

____

____

MAIN AND SUPPORTING IDEAS

4 Why are there so many storage facilities in North America?

____

____

5 List five sharing economy companies that are mentioned in this text.

____

____

6 What types of companies are losing money because of the sharing economy? List at least three types.

____

____

7 What are advantages of the sharing economy? List two or three advantages.

____

____

8 What is the most important "currency" in the sharing economy? See paragraph 7. ____________

WRITING

Write a paragraph presenting your opinion of the sharing economy.

WATCHING 3.3 Consumer Power

In the spring of 2008, Dave Carroll flew to Nebraska with his band. His guitar did not survive the journey. He created a revenge video called *My Broken Guitar*. The video went viral on YouTube, with over three million views in ten days.

COMPREHENSION

1 What is the name of Carroll's band?

a. Sam's Dream b. Carroll's Boys c. Sons of Maxwell

2 What is the name of Dave Carroll's song? ____________

3 Describe what happened to Carroll. Use the past tense.

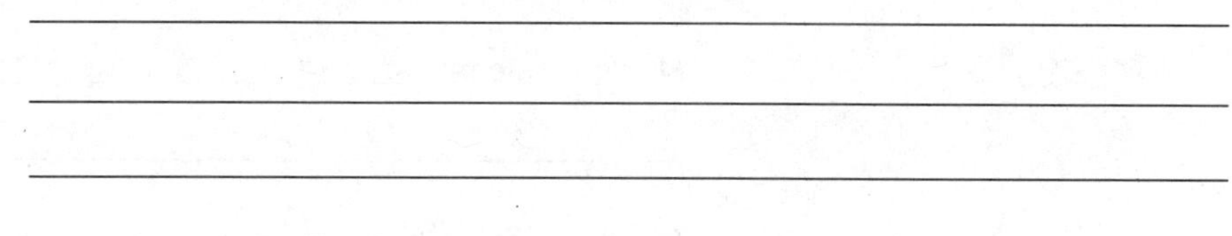

Dave Carroll

4 How many songs does Carroll intend to write about the broken guitar?

a. one b. two c. three

5 What can we learn from Dave Carroll's experience?

____

____

____

____

DISCUSSION

1 Why did so many people watch *My Broken Guitar* on YouTube? Think of some reasons the video became popular.

2 How is YouTube helping consumers?

SPEAKING Interview about Trends

Discuss the following questions with a partner. Then write your partner's answers on the lines.

Partner's name: ______________________________

Discussing the Past

1 During your childhood, what were the most popular fashions? You can describe hair, clothing, and shoe styles for men and women.

Men's fashions: ______________________________

____

Women's fashions: ______________________________

____

2 During your childhood, what technological products were popular? Describe them. ______________________________

____

3 When you were a child, what were your favourite toys? List at least three items. ______________________________

____

Discussing the Present

4 What styles are popular today? Think about hair, clothing, and shoe styles for men and women.

Men's fashions: ______________________________

____

Women's fashions: ______________________________

____

5 What technological products do people use today? List at least five items.

____

____

6 What are your favourite items? List at least three things. Explain why they are your favourites. ______________________________

____

WRITING

Write an essay about trends in the past and in the present. Include information from your partner's answers in your essay.

TAKE ACTION!

WRITING TOPICS

Write about one of the following topics. For information about paragraph and essay structure, see the Writing Workshops on pages 137-150.

1 Personal Style

Describe your style and the style of someone you know. Write two paragraphs.

- In your first paragraph, describe yourself. What are you wearing right now? What clothes or fashions do you like or dislike? Where do you shop? Give examples.
- In your second paragraph, describe a friend or family member. What is he or she wearing today? What is that person's style? What type of shopper is that person?

2 Favourite Objects

Discuss items that are important to you.

- First, discuss a very important object that you loved when you were a child. Describe the object using descriptive vocabulary.
- In your second paragraph, write about an object that is important to you today. It can be anything that you own and value.
- In your conclusion, make a prediction. Explain what possession will be the most important to you. Think of something you currently own that will keep its value.

3 Brands

A brand is a name or trademark of a product or service. For example, *Apple*, *Nike*, and *Heinz* are brands. Write about popular brands and your personal preferences.

- In a short introduction, explain why people buy certain brands.
- In your second paragraph, describe a time in the past when you bought something because it was popular. For example, did you buy a particular brand of running shoes or a certain kind of cellphone? Was it a good or bad decision to buy that item? Explain why.
- In your third paragraph, discuss your current favourite brands. For instance, think about shoe, computer, car, or clothing brands. Why are some brands so popular? Why do you like certain brands? If you do not buy particular brands, explain why.
- In a short conclusion, make a prediction or a suggestion.

SPEAKING TOPICS

Prepare a presentation about one of the following topics.

1 What Is Happening Now?

Look in your photo album or online for a picture that contains the following elements. You can look on flickr.com or any photo website.

- There must be at least three people in the picture.
- The people must be doing different actions.
- The people must be in an identifiable place.
- Invent a story about the people in the picture. Use the simple present and the present progressive tenses in your story.

Example: The man's name is Thomas. He works in a bank. He is talking with his girlfriend, Julia. Julia is laughing because ...

2 Dragons' Den

(Optional: Work with a partner or a team of students.)

Think of a new fashion or product and propose it to *Dragons' Den*. As a suggestion, you can combine two pieces of clothing into one or combine two products into one. Be prepared to include the following aspects in your talk:

- Explain who you are marketing your product to.
- Determine a price for your product.
- Determine a value for your company. Then decide how much money you need to ask for.
- Describe the best features of your item.
- Explain what you are doing these days to promote your item. (Use your imagination.)

You must answer questions about your product. You will also ask other team members about their products. Your team will have a chance to be both the inventors and the dragons.

3 Trends

A trend is something that is very popular for a short period of time. Speak about trends in the past, present, and future.

- Describe a trend that was popular during your childhood. It could be a clothing, shoe, or hair fashion. Or, you can describe a product such as a game, car, or technological item. Choose something that was very popular for a short period of time.
- Describe a current trend. It could be an item of clothing, a style of shoes, or a hair fashion. Or, you can describe a product such as a game, car, or technological item. Choose something that is very popular these days.
- Predict a future trend. What will everyone buy next year?

SPEAKING PRESENTATION

TIPS

- **Practise your presentation and time yourself.** You should speak for about two minutes (or for a length determined by your teacher).
- **Use cue cards.** Do not read! Put about fifteen keywords on your cue cards.
- **Bring visual support**, such as a picture, photograph, object, video, or PowerPoint slides.
- **Classmates will ask you questions about your presentation.** You must also ask your classmates about their presentations. Review how to form questions before your presentation day.

To practise vocabulary from this chapter, visit My eLab.

REVISING AND EDITING

REVISE FOR TRANSITIONS

A good paragraph should have transition words to link ideas. The following paragraph does not flow because it has no transitions. Add the appropriate words in the spaces. Choose from the following transition words. (To learn more about transition words and phrases, see Writing Workshop 3 on page 148.)

~~first~~	finally	of course	then
for example	in fact	to conclude	

I am changing my spending habits. ___First___, I destroyed my credit cards. ____________, I put my MasterCard and my Bay card in the shredder last week. __________ I made a budget. ______________, I do not always stick to my budget, but I try to. ____________, I will sell old items before I buy any new ones. ________________, if I want a new iPhone, I must sell other items until I have enough to buy the iPhone. ________________, I am really making an effort to change and to consume less.

EDIT PRESENT PROGRESSIVE VERBS

Practise editing a student paragraph. Underline and correct five errors with present progressive verbs, not including the example.

Right now, I ^am wearing Nike runners. Melissa is carry a purse with a Calvin Klein logo, and Samuel is having the slogan "I love my iPhone" on his T-shirt. We promoting some brands. Of course, we is not trying to advertise products, but people see what we wearing. We may argue that brands don't matter. However, advertising influences our buying choices.

GRAMMAR TIP

Use Complete Verbs

With present progressive verbs, use the correct form of the verb *be* (*am*, *are*, *is*). Also, ensure that the main verb ends in *-ing*.

She ^is buying some new shoes. Her friends are ~~wait~~ waiting for her.

To learn more about the present progressive tense, see Unit 3 in *Avenues1: English Grammar.*

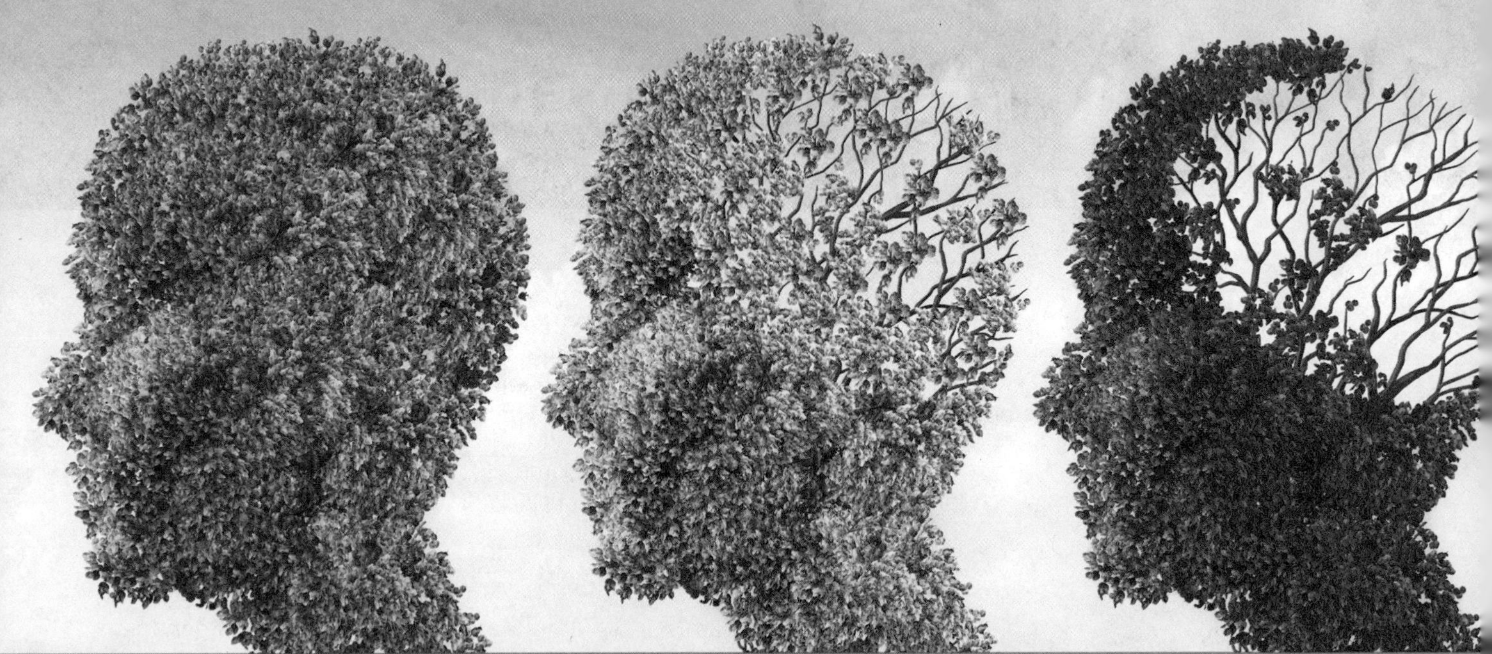

"There are lots of people who mistake their imagination for their memory."

— CESARE PAVESE

CHAPTER 4

MEMORIES OF OUR LIVES

We spend much of our present thinking about the past. What are the benefits of having a good memory? In this chapter, you will learn about memory, and you will also reflect on human stories.

Memory Games

Past Recollections

Work with a partner or a small team of classmates. Take turns chatting about the following topics. You can change topics at any time. When the teacher flicks the lights, change speakers.

1. My earliest childhood memory
2. What I did last Saturday (provide details)
3. What I had for lunch yesterday (provide details)

Memory Games

Try the following memory games. Your teacher will guide you through the activities.

1 A loonie is a $1 coin. Which image shows the real Canadian loonie? Do not cheat and look at a coin! Make a guess based on your memories of handling coins every day.

a.

b.

c.

d.

e.

2 You probably use your smartphone every day. Without looking at your phone, answer the following questions about it. Use your memory.

What icon is at the bottom right corner? ____________________

What icon is at the top right corner? ____________________

3 Look at this page. Do **not** look up. Describe what your teacher is wearing.

____

____

____

4 For fifteen seconds, look at the following list of words. Then close your book and listen to your teacher read out a list of words. Were some of those words on the list you just looked at?

dream tired dark star moon bed pillow bedroom

WATCHING 4.1 Memory Wizards

Imagine being able to remember every day of your life. Lesley Stahl reports on people with remarkable memories.

COMPREHENSION

PART 1

1 The scientist who first discovered remarkable memory is Dr. James McGaugh. What university does he work at?

a. University of Calgary
b. Boston University
c. University of California
d. University of Arizona

2 When *60 Minutes* did an earlier story about memory, scientists knew of how many people with remarkable memories?

a. six b. twenty c. fifty d. fifty-six

3 On what day of the week did the first *60 Minutes* story about memory appear?

a. Saturday b. Sunday c. Monday d. Friday

4 Describe the "memory wizards." How are they different from other people?

____

____

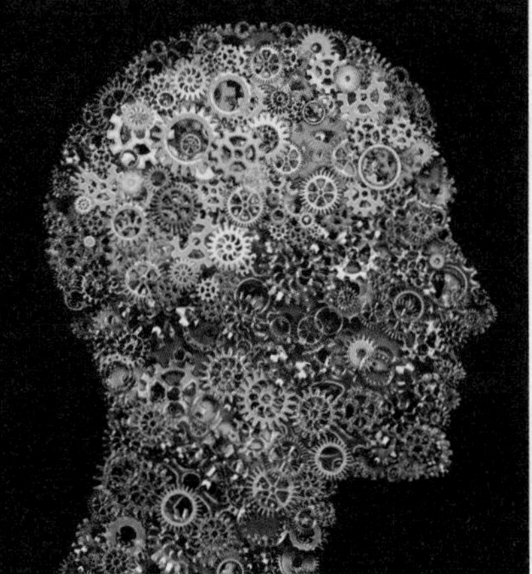

5 What is true about memory wizards? Choose two answers.

___ When they hear a date, they know what day of the week it was.

___ When they think of a day in the distant past, they relive the emotions of that day.

___ They only remember emotional days in the past. They forget boring days.

6 Joe DeGrandis showed classmates his amazing memory at . . ..

a. a science fair b. a birthday party c. a magic show

7 How old was Jake Housler when his family first realized that he was different?

a. three b. five c. ten d. fifteen

PART 2

8 According to the video, how many children, other than Jake, have an amazing memory? __________

9 Chad and Tyler are twins. Do they both have remarkable memories?

☐ Yes ☐ No

10 People with amazing memories viewed a film about a dinner party. When the doctor asked them questions, what happened?

a. They remembered every detail.
b. They did not perform better than the average person.

11 Can average people remember yesterday as well as people with superior memories?

☐ Yes ☐ No

12 The memory wizards are not exceptional learners; they are poor . . ..

a. forgetters b. students c. teachers

13 What is a disadvantage of having a superior memory? ____________________

____

14 How does Louise Owen feel about her remarkable memory? ______________

____

DISCUSSION

Work with a partner, and discuss if you would like to be able to remember everything. Explain why or why not.

VOCABULARY **BOOST**

Remember, Memory, Souvenir, and Memoir

Remember is a verb. It means "keep something in mind; not forget."

I **remember** the accident. It happened during a storm.

Memory is a noun. It refers to the capacity to recall things or to the recollection of past events.

I have an accurate **memory**. That horrible accident is a bad **memory**.

A ***souvenir*** is a memento that you buy or give as a reminder of a special place or event.

I bought a **souvenir** in Banff. I bought a small Canadian flag.

A ***memoir*** is a true story—an autobiography—that you write about your experiences.

Barack Obama wrote a **memoir** about his childhood in Hawaii.

PRACTICE

Fill in the blank(s) in each sentence with the correct word(s). Choose one of the words from this list. Remember to add -s to the noun or verb, if needed.

remember memory souvenir memoir

1 Alanis ________________ trivial details about the past. She has an amazing ______________.

2 Many years ago, Alanis visited Banff. She bought a ______________: a tiny plastic bear. Alanis ______________ many details about the bear. She has some great ______________ of the trip.

3 When she becomes famous, Alanis will write a ______________ about her life. She travels extensively, so it will be interesting.

READING 4.1

WHAT IS YOUR EARLIEST CHILDHOOD MEMORY? Do you remember your baby years? Read about childhood memories to discover some answers.

Why Childhood Memories Disappear

BY ALASDAIR WILKINS

1 My first memory is of the day my brother was born: November 14, 1991. My father drove my grandparents and me over to the hospital. I recall my mother's hospital room, and I recall gazing at my only sibling in his bedside **cot**. But mostly, I remember what was on the television: the final two minutes of a *Thomas the Tank Engine* episode. I even remember the precise story. Research suggests that people's memories often begin with significant personal events. First memories also date to when they are about three and a half years old. That was my age when my brother was born.

cot: small bed

My eLab

You can prepare for your reading tests by trying the reading strategies on pages 132-136. You can also practise by visiting My eLab. Click on Reading Strategies to find a variety of exercises.

2 Carole Peterson, a professor of psychology at Memorial University of Newfoundland, studies children's memories. "Children have a very good memory system. But whether or not something hangs around long-term depends on several other factors," Peterson said. Two of the most important factors are whether the memory "has emotion infused in it" and whether the memory is coherent. Does the remembered story make sense when we recall it later?

3 Story-based "episodic" memory is not the only kind of memory. Steven Reznick, a professor at the University of North Carolina, says that shortly after birth, infants start forming impressions of faces and react when they see those faces again; this is "recognition" memory. The ability to understand words and learn language relies on working memory, which kicks in at around six months old. More sophisticated forms of memory develop in the second year as the child retains concepts.

4 For memories to endure, we need to understand the concepts that give meaning to an event. For the memory of my brother's birth, I have to understand concepts like "hospital," "brother," and "cot." Then, for the memory to remain accessible, my younger self had to remember those concepts in the same language-based way that my adult self remembers information. Earlier memories used more rudimentary, pre-verbal **means**. Those memories become unreachable because the acquisition of language reshapes how our minds work.

means: methods

5 To see how well my first memory held up, I called my dad to verify the details. I worried that I had invented my grandparents' presence, but he confirmed that they had flown over from England for the occasion. He also confirmed my brother's cot and the television, but he disputed one vital detail. He spoke with the precision of a former doctor: "I won't say with any confidence that *Thomas the Tank Engine* was on the TV." Still, we agreed that a three-year-old would be more likely to remember such a detail than the father of a newborn baby.

6 The randomness of that detail makes me think it's plausible. False memories exist, but their construction appears to begin much later in life. As for why older children and adults begin to fill in **gaps** in their memories with invented details, Peterson pointed out that memory is a fundamentally constructive activity. We use it to build understanding of the world, and that sometimes requires more complete narratives than our memories can recall by themselves. As people get older, it becomes easier to **conflate** actual memories with other stimuli.

gaps: spaces

conflate: join or mix together

7 Reznick told me of a distinct memory he has of riding with his sister in a toy wagon. The problem is that he doesn't remember doing it as much as he remembers *seeing* himself do it. He discovered why when he found an old

photograph of him and his sister in that wagon. He forgot about the photograph but remembered what it depicted, so over time the picture became its own memory.

fade: start to disappear; lose detail

8 So what do we leave behind as our earliest memories **fade**? In my case, I lost an entire country. My family emigrated from England in June 1991, when I was about three years old, so I have no memories of Chester, my birthplace. I grew up knowing England through imported foods and TV shows and my parents' accents. I knew England as a culture, but not as a place.

9 Memories—even the ones we forgot long ago—shape us. In 2012, I travelled to the west of England to see my birthplace. I was in Chester for less than a day, but there was something *right* about that little city. The feeling was unmistakable: I was home. Was my brain simply attaching outsize importance to Chester because my adult self knew its significance, or were these feelings caused by genuine memories? Reznick says it could be "recognition memory." Associations with my hometown that I formed as an infant could endure.

(746 words)

Source:
Wilkins, Alasdair. "Why Childhood Memories Disappear." *The Atlantic*. Atlantic Monthly Group, 6 Jul. 2015. Web.

COMPREHENSION

VOCABULARY

1 Match the words or phrases with the definitions. Use context clues. The paragraph numbers are in parentheses.

Terms		Definitions
1. gazing at (1)	____	a. stays; continues
2. hangs around (2)	____	b. remained true and possible
3. kicks in (3)	____	c. looking at
4. held up (5)	____	d. begins

2 Find a word in paragraph 3 that means "babies." ______________

GENERAL UNDERSTANDING

3 What type of memory do babies and children under the age of two have?

a. They have no memories.

b. They can remember faces and recognize things.

c. They can remember events.

4 What causes memories to form and endure in children over the age of three?

____

____

5 Basically, why do people forget their baby years?

a. Those memories are pre-verbal, so people can't recall or retell them.

b. Babies and small children do not remember things.

c. Nothing significant happens during those early years, so there is no reason to remember them.

My eLab

Answer additional reading and listening questions in My eLab. You can also access audio and video clips online.

6 Why does the writer have no clear memories of his birthplace?

____

____

7 The writer returned to his birthplace of Chester, England. What happened?

a. He remembered specific people and places.

b. Something felt right about the place. Possibly, he had recognition memory of the place.

c. He remembered specific events in his early childhood, such as the birth of his brother.

d. He did not remember the place.

WRITING

Write about one of your earliest childhood memories. Where were you? What happened?

VOCABULARY **BOOST**

Family

Work with a partner. Put the letter of the correct definition in the space provided.

Terms		Definitions
1. spouse	____	a. child with no brothers or sisters
2. mother-in-law	____	b. your father's wife (She has no biological connection to you.)
3. stepmother	____	c. your brother who shares one parent with you
4. only child	____	d. your spouse's mother
5. twins	____	e. two children born on the same date by the same mother
6. half brother	____	f. your stepparent's son (He is not biologically related to you.)
7. stepbrother	____	g. marital partner (*Husband* refers to a male, and *wife* refers to a female.)

My eLab

Visit My eLab to practise more vocabulary, such as family-related words.

SPEAKING Birth Order and Childhood Memories

When you remember your childhood, do you recall good times with your brothers or sisters? Do you have stepsisters or stepbrothers, or are you an only child? Our sibling relationships last longer than any other relationship—from our birth until death.

There are also many studies that suggest that birth order affects personality. Look at the following personality traits. With your partner, assign each characteristic to the appropriate child in a family. If any terms are unfamiliar, use your dictionary.

perfectionist	high achiever	risk taker	jealous
spoiled	flexible	selfish	responsible

Oldest child	**Middle child**	**Youngest child**
____________	____________	____________
____________	____________	____________
____________	____________	____________

WRITING

Write about your best childhood memories. Are you the youngest, oldest, or middle child? Do you have stepsisters or stepbrothers? Are you an only child? Explain how the presence or absence of siblings affected your childhood.

WHICH IS MORE IMPORTANT: INTELLIGENCE OR HARD WORK? Read about Marley Montour's lazy years.

GRAMMAR LINK

In paragraphs 1 to 4, fill in the blanks with the correct past tense forms of the verbs in parentheses. You can listen to the essay in My eLab and correct your answers. While you are listening, pay attention to the speaker's intonation and pronunciation.

My Lazy Years

BY MARLEY MONTOUR

My eLab

You can prepare for your reading tests by trying the reading strategies on pages 132-136. You can also practise by visiting My eLab. Click on Reading Strategies to find a variety of exercises.

humble: modest

1 While I was growing up, my parents praised me for my intelligence. My teachers complained that I often (have) ________ my "head in the clouds," but my marks (be) ________ excellent. My report cards contained the comments "gifted" and "brilliant student." My proud parents (brag) ____________ about me to their friends. In my final year of elementary school, at the age of twelve, I (win) ________ awards in math and English. I could succeed without even trying! I was a genius! As a result, I was not a **humble** child, and I was not alone. According to a Columbia University survey, 85 percent of parents believe that they should praise their children for their intelligence. But in the real world, intelligence is not as important as a strong work ethic.

floundered: struggled; had difficulty

doodled: drew little pictures

2 Although I received top marks in elementary school, I **floundered** when I reached high school. Class work (become) ____________ more complex. Because I was so "smart," I (think) ____________ I could continue to succeed without effort. I put off assignments to hang out with friends. In class, I **doodled**

in my notebooks and daydreamed. I could pass my finals if I crammed at the end of each semester. Naturally, my grades (drop) ______________, and many of my classmates surpassed me. Over time, I (stop) ______________ believing that I was very smart, and I barely graduated from high school.

eke by: succeed

3 When I got to college, nobody forced me to go to class or do homework. Teachers (care + not) ________________ if I passed or mostly failed. I (feel) _________ bored, smoked too much weed, and didn't try to **eke by** anymore. It seemed like there was a wide world to explore, and class was the least interesting part of it.

bright: intelligent

4 When the college threatened to expel me for too many failed classes, I took a break from school. I dropped out for a year to explore the glamorous, fast-paced world of flipping burgers and cleaning public washrooms. During one of my shifts at work, when I was elbow deep in a toilet, I realized that I wanted more in my life. I returned for my last year of college, but I still did the minimal amount of work. I just didn't know how to work hard. When former classmates—who were not very **bright**—got accepted into tough university programs, I was jealous and resentful.

5 "You are so smart," my parents lamented. "Why did you lose your way?" I'm not alone. Apparently, the world is full of people who have a decent IQ but a very poor work ethic. The reasons, it turns out, may go back to the way we think about ourselves and our beliefs about intelligence.

6 A strong work ethic surpasses intelligence when it comes to success. Stanford psychologist Carol Dweck did research to determine the importance of certain types of reinforcement. She divided Grade 5 students into two groups. Students in the first group did some tests and received praise for being "very smart." When they tried a more difficult test, many of them gave up and said, "I'm not so smart after all."

7 The second group was told, "You worked very hard at these problems." They learned that intelligence is like a muscle, and when they exercise that muscle, it grows stronger. Students in the second group also struggled with the more difficult test. However, they stated that they just needed to work harder. They kept trying to solve the problems, and they had better scores than the first "intelligent" group.

8 Dweck was surprised by how large the effect was. When teachers emphasize effort, children have a variable that they can manage and "see themselves as in control of their success. Emphasizing natural intelligence takes it out of the child's control, and it provides no good recipe for responding to a failure," said Dweck, in an interview with the *New York Times*.

9 When I look back, I don't dwell on regrets. During my high school and college years, I was exposed to new ideas and people. I discovered what I liked, and things—um, elbow deep in a toilet—that I really, really disliked. Now that I value effort, I can work hard on a career plan. I just have to figure out what that is.

(695 words)

COMPRESSION

VOCABULARY

1 Some of the following expressions are idiomatic: their meanings do not necessarily match the meanings of the individual words. Look at each of the following expressions in context. Write the letter of the best definition in the space provided. The paragraph number is in parentheses.

Terms		**Definitions**
1. had my head in the clouds (1)	_____	a. quickly prepared for an exam at the last minute
2. hang out (2)	_____	b. arms are submerged in something
3. crammed (2)	_____	c. left before completing school
4. dropped out (4)	_____	d. find the answer to a question
5. elbow deep (4)	_____	e. was distracted, not focused
6. figure out (9)	_____	f. spend time with (someone)

2 Which two words indicate "a student's proficiency in a test or course"? Circle two answers. (For help, see paragraphs 1 and 2.)

a. notes b. marks c. grades

MAIN IDEAS AND MAIN MESSAGE

3 Why did Marley Montour feel so intelligent? ______________________

____

____

4 What happened to Montour in high school? ______________________

____

____

5 How did Montour's self-perception change over time? ______________________

____

____

____

6 Why did Montour drop out of college? ______________________

____

____

7 What is the main message? What lesson does this essay contain?

____

____

____

WRITING

Write about your childhood education and your work ethic. What type of student were you? Did you believe that you were intelligent? Did you make mistakes? Are you a different type of student now? Include specific details to support your points.

SPEAKING Life-Changing Event

PART 1 Discuss Proverbs

A proverb is a short saying that effectively expresses a common truth about life. Work with a partner or a small team, and discuss the following proverbs. What do they mean?

1 Don't judge a book by its cover.

2 Practice makes perfect.

3 The early bird catches the worm.

4 Half a loaf is better than none.

5 People who live in glass houses should not throw stones.

6 Let sleeping dogs lie.

PART 2 Presentation

Present an experience that changed your life. Choose an experience that illustrates one of the proverbs you just discussed or another proverb that you know.

To get ideas, ask yourself the following questions about the past.

- Did you ever hurt someone or help someone?
- Did you or someone you know ever make a mistake or a bad decision?
- Did you or someone you know ever make a very good decision?
- Did something really positive or really negative happen to you at school? How did it affect you?
- Did an important world event have an impact on you?

Structure your presentation in the following way.

- First, explain what happened. Use the past tense, and provide specific details.
- Then, explain how the event changed you or someone you know. How are you or that person different today?
- In your conclusion, explain what you will teach your children. End with a proverb.

GRAMMAR TIP

Past Tense Verbs

Generally use the simple past (*went*, *ate*, *thought*, etc.) to describe past events. Do not use the past progressive (*was going*) unless the past action was clearly in progress.

Everyday, I ~~was playing~~ played at the construction site, and I ~~was taking~~ took risks.

For more information about past tense verbs, see Units 4 and 7 in *Avenues 1: English Grammar.*

WATCHING 4.2 Humans of New York

A few years ago, Brandon Stanton began to document the lives of typical people in New York. Watch and then answer the questions.

WRITTEN COMPREHENSION

Write a paragraph about Brandon Stanton. Include the following information.

- What does Brandon try to accomplish through his photos? What is his goal?
- How does he approach people?
- Where does he put his photos?
- Why are his photos popular?

WRITING Photo Memories

Choose three photos of people in your life. Insert the photos in a document. Under each photo, write a short paragraph about the person. Tell a little story about that person's life. Choose events that you consider the most important.

OPTION: If you feel brave enough, take photographs of three students in your college or of three strangers. Ask each person a few questions, and write at least five sentences under each photo.

READING 4.3 The Silent Generation

Ruth Wade was born in 1934 in Medicine Hat, Alberta. She came of age in the 1940s and early 1950s. Her generation, sometimes called the Silent Generation, had particular qualities. In the interview, Wade discusses various characteristics of her generation.

The Silent Generation

AN INTERVIEW WITH RUTH WADE

1 **How did World War II[1] impact your childhood?**

2 I was five years old when the war began. The war was far away but it affected us. I worried about people who went to fight. Our neighbour, Johnny, was cool, and he often talked to us. He was only nineteen years old when he died fighting overseas.

1 World War II occurred from 1939 to 1945.

My eLab

You can prepare for your reading tests by trying the reading strategies on pages 132-136. You can also practise by visiting My eLab. Click on Reading Strategies to find a variety of exercises.

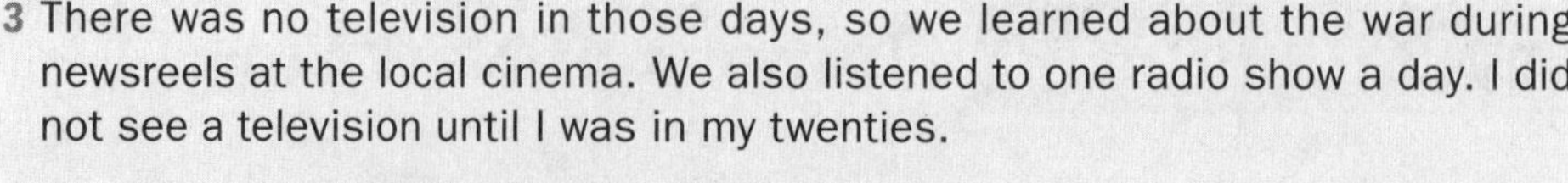

3 There was no television in those days, so we learned about the war during newsreels at the local cinema. We also listened to one radio show a day. I did not see a television until I was in my twenties.

4 **During your youth, how did teenagers rebel?**

5 Probably the riskiest thing we did was have drag races. On country roads, guys would race each other. A few bad accidents happened. Cars did not have seatbelts, so drag races were pretty risky.

6 Also, some youths tried to stand out and look different. Most young men had short hair, but some got Mohawks. They were considered pretty hip. Later, in the 1950s, when Elvis Presley was popular, guys had ducktails. They would let the hair grow long over the ears and keep it shorter on top. My brother had a ducktail and my father hated it. Dad often threatened to cut off the ducktail while my brother was sleeping.

7 In the 1940s, our parents wore hats when they went out shopping or whatever. My generation stopped wearing hats. Maybe the boys were too worried about their hair.

8 **How was family life different during the 1950s?**

9 Divorce was rare. Even when marriages were very violent or horrible, couples usually stayed together. Most people had at least four or five children. Families were united. On weekends, the whole family would go to dances or play card games, and the babies would sleep in the corner.

10 **How were single mothers treated in those years?**

11 It was terrible for girls who got pregnant. One girl I knew had a baby when she was fifteen. She was a really nice, quiet girl. After she had the baby, everybody shunned her. Nobody wanted to associate with her. They also treated her son badly just because he had no father. Sometimes, to avoid a scandal, the girl's parents would pretend that the baby was theirs.

12 **Was abortion an option during those decades—the 1940s and 1950s?**

13 In those days, abortion was illegal[2]. Of course, backstreet abortions happened, and sometimes the girls got sick or died. They used coat hangers, and conditions were unsanitary. There was another terrible thing that women did. Sometimes, women ate a small amount of gopher poison to provoke an abortion. The poison would cause a miscarriage.

14 People don't realize how difficult it was for girls in the past. Unwed mothers were called **tramps** and ostracized, so girls were really scared to get pregnant.

tramps: promiscuous women (derogatory term)

15 **How were gender roles different?**

16 Well, women worked in factories during the early 1940s because the men went off to war. However, there was a law that when the men came back at the end of the war, employers had to give the jobs to the veterans. At our local glass factory, the women were **fired** when the men returned. It was fair, I think, because those veterans needed their jobs.

fired: removed from their jobs

2 In Canada, nineteenth-century legislation outlawed abortion. In 1988, Canada's Supreme Court ruled that the law was unconstitutional. Currently, there is no law against abortion.

17 Girls usually didn't continue schooling, but my father was rare, and he encouraged me to go to university. I received a scholarship and did one year at university before I got married.

18 **How old were you when you got married?**

old maid: insulting term for an unmarried woman

19 I was nineteen. If a girl was twenty-five and single, people would call her an "**old maid**." My marriage was controversial because my family was Protestant, and I married a Catholic. Some family members refused to come to my wedding. People were more religious, but they were also more intolerant.

20 I had four children, but I was very bored being a housewife. So, when my youngest child was in school, I took a job teaching. Some neighbours insulted my husband by saying things such as, "I guess you can't afford to support your wife." It was difficult for us because women were expected to stay home and take care of the family.

(711 words)

COMPREHENSION

MAIN AND SUPPORTING IDEAS

What are the main features of Ruth Wade's youth? Complete the chart with descriptions of various aspects of life for people of the Silent Generation.

Politics War: Laws:
Technology
Family Life
Gender Roles
Religion

WRITING

Using a separate sheet of paper, do the following.

1. Identify five difficult words in the text. Write a definition for each word.
2. Write five more questions that you would like to ask Ruth.
3. In a paragraph of about 120 words, write about the Silent Generation. Mention at least five key features of this generation. Use your own words. Do not copy exact phrases from the text.

LISTENING PRACTICE

1. Pronounce Past Tense Verbs

Regular past tense verbs end in *-ed*. There are three different ways to pronounce the final *-ed* ending.

PRONUNCIATION TIP

Regular Past Tense Verbs

Rules	Past Tense Ending Sounds Like	Examples		
When the verb ends in an *-s*, *-k*, *-f*, *-p*, *-x*, *-ch*, or *-sh* sound, the final *-ed* is pronounced *-t*.	t	asked	kissed	wished
When the verb ends in *-t* or *-d*, the final *-ed* is pronounced as a separate syllable.	id	wanted	added	folded
In all other regular verbs, the final *-ed* is pronounced *-d*.	d	lived	aged	moved

Repeat each verb twice after the speaker. Then indicate if the verb ends with a *-t*, a *-d*, or an *-id* sound.

Example: added t d (id)

1 asked t d id

2 needed t d id

3 discussed t d id

4 opened t d id

5 divided t d id

6 missed t d id

7 counted t d id

8 baked t d id

9 tried t d id

10 landed t d id

2. Pronounce Sentences and Identify Verbs

Review how to pronounce certain irregular past tense verbs.

PRONUNCIATION TIP

Irregular Past Tense Verbs

Rule	Sound	Examples		
When the past tense verb ends in *-ought* or *-aught*, pronounce the final letters as *-ot*.	ot	bought	taught	caught

Repeat each sentence after the speaker. Then fill in the blanks with the missing verbs.

1 We ______________ into the woods.

2 My father ______________ a lot of camping supplies.

3 We ______________ to build a fire.

4 We went to a lake and ______________ some fish.

5 During the night, we ______________ that there was a strange sound.

6 My brother ______________ outside and saw a bear.

7 He ______________ my father a question.

8 My father ______________ that we stay completely still.

9 We were scared, so we ______________ the seconds.

10 The next day, my brother ______________ to leave.

LISTENING Coming of Age in the 1990s

Natalia Kosek was born in 1982, and she came of age in the 1990s. Natalia discusses her generation.

COMPREHENSION

Are the following sentences true or false? Circle *T* for "true" or *F* for "false."

1 Natalia's generation did not have to fight for women's rights. T F

2 Generation Y is more politically active than the previous generation. T F

3 Natalia had a cellphone when she was a little girl. T F

4 Natalia first used the Internet when she was at the end of high school. T F

5 What were three problems or inconveniences with the early Internet?

____

____

____

6 What was the most popular musical style for Generation Y?

a. punk b. grunge c. rap d. techno

7 According to Natalia, what were some fashion trends in the 1990s? Choose four answers.

___ black hats
___ Converse running shoes
___ ball chains
___ neck tattoos
___ ripped jeans
___ long white dresses
___ platform shoes
___ oversized flannel shirts

8 What world events shaped Natalia's generation? Name three events.

____

____

9 What is the main worry facing Generation Y?

a. war b. the environment c. unemployment d. drugs

10 What did Natalia study at university? ______________________________

SPEAKING The Current Generation

Discuss the current generation. Fill in the chart with information.

Political and Social Issues (List five problems that concern your generation.)

____

Technology

____

Music

____

Family Life

____

Religion

TAKE ACTION!

WRITING TOPICS

Write about one of the following topics. For information about essay structure, see Writing Workshop 2 on pages 144-147.

1 Childhood

In My eLab, read "My Childhood in Somalia." Compare your childhood to that of children in Somalia. In one paragraph, describe your childhood. In a second paragraph, describe Mawlid's childhood.

2 Generations

Describe your generation and another generation. You can discuss the Silent Generation, Generation Y, or your parents' generation.

- In a short introduction, write general sentences that introduce your topic.
- In your first body paragraph, describe a past generation. If you choose a generation that was described in this chapter, do not use exact words or phrases from the text. Use your own words.
- In your second body paragraph, describe your generation. What makes it unique? Use examples from your life.
- Conclude with a suggestion or prediction.

3 Memories

Write about two of your strongest childhood memories. Write a paragraph about each event. When you finish, check your past tense verbs.

SPEAKING TOPICS

Prepare a presentation on one of the following topics.

1 People in My World

Take photographs of five significant people in your life. In a presentation of about two minutes, describe the people in the photos. Explain something about each person. What is unique or interesting about that person? How is the person related to you? How did that person help you or affect you?

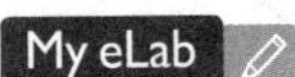

To practise vocabulary from this chapter, visit My eLab.

2 My Biggest Role Models

Discuss people who influenced you in the past and those who influence you today.

- In a short introduction, explain why people need heroes and role models.
- Discuss your heroes when you were a child. Who did you admire? You can talk about real people or about fictional heroes such as Superman.
- Then describe one or more people who influence you today. Why do you admire them?

SPEAKING PRESENTATION TIPS

- **Practise your presentation and time yourself.** You should speak for about two minutes (or for a length of time determined by your teacher).
- **Use cue cards.** Do not read! Put about fifteen keywords on your cue cards.
- **Bring visual support,** such as a picture, photograph, object, video, or PowerPoint slides.
- **Classmates will ask you questions about your presentation.** You must also ask your classmates about their presentations. Review how to form questions before your presentation day.

REVISING AND EDITING

REVISE FOR SUPPORTING DETAILS

A good paragraph should include supporting details. Practice revising a student paragraph. Add examples and anecdotes to make the paragraph more complete.

During our school years, we learn important lessons. First, we learn how to socialize. ____

____

____

We also learn important work-related skills. ________________________

____

____

Finally, we discover our interests and passions. ______________________

____

____

We should appreciate our college education.

EDIT PAST TENSE VERBS

Practise editing a student paragraph. Underline and correct six verb tense errors, not including the example.

When I was a child, I loved nature. My stepfather had a cottage, and we <u>go</u> (went) there during school breaks. At the cottage, we didn't had access to the Internet. What we do? We walked in the forest. We swum in the lake. We played board games, and we builded a fort in the trees. We sometimes saw wild animals. Also, we taked our dog for walks every night, even if it was cold outside. We was never bored. Five years ago, when my stepfather sold the cottage, we felt sad.

To learn more about paragraph and essay writing, see the Writing Workshops on pages 137-150.

GRAMMAR TIP

Was or *Were*

In the past tense, use **was** when the subject is *I*, *he*, *she*, or *it*. Use **were** when the subject is *you*, *we*, or *they*.

We ~~was~~ were busy when we stayed at the cottage.

CHAPTER **5**

AROUND THE WORLD

"Travel makes us modest. We see what a tiny place we occupy in the world."

— GUSTAVE FLAUBERT, FRENCH WRITER

Why do people travel? What are the benefits of learning about other cultural traditions? In this chapter, you will read about travelling and cultural traditions.

START UP Name That Country

Travel Talk

Work with a small group. Take turns chatting about different types of travel shown in the following photos.

- Which type of accommodations do you prefer? Explain why.
- What kind of travel does each photo suggest? Discuss the advantages and disadvantages of the different types of trips.

When the teacher flicks the lights on and off, change speakers.

beach hut

couch surfing in someone's home

tent

sailboat

youth hostel (shared room)

hotel in a big city

Name That Country

Work with a team of students. View the list of cities. Then indicate the names of the countries where these cities are located. Also write the nationalities. If you are not sure, you can guess.

Delhi

	Cities	Country	Nationality
	Example: Paris, Lyon, Marseilles	France	French
1	Madrid, Barcelona, Seville		
2	Zurich, Geneva, Lausanne		
3	Athens, Sparta, Naxos		
4	Johannesburg, Capetown, Mbombela		
5	Sydney, Brisbane, Melbourne		
6	Chicago, Dallas, Seattle		
7	Frankfurt, Hamburg, Berlin		
8	Edinburgh, Glasgow, Aberdeen		
9	Moscow, St. Petersburg, Ufa		
10	Dublin, Cork, Galway		
11	Vancouver, Toronto, Montréal		
12	Rio de Janiero, Brasilia, Sao Paulo		
13	Delhi, Mumbai, Madras		
14	Acapulco, Cancun, Tijuana		
15	Beijing, Shanghai, Guangzhou		

DISCUSSION

List any two countries you would like to visit. Speak with a partner and explain why.

GRAMMAR TIP

Using *The*

Do not put *the* before most city and country names. Some exceptions are *the United States*, *the Netherlands*, and *the Dominican Republic*.

I visited Brazil, China, Australia, and Ireland.

To learn more about articles, see Unit 5 in *Avenues 1: English Grammar.*

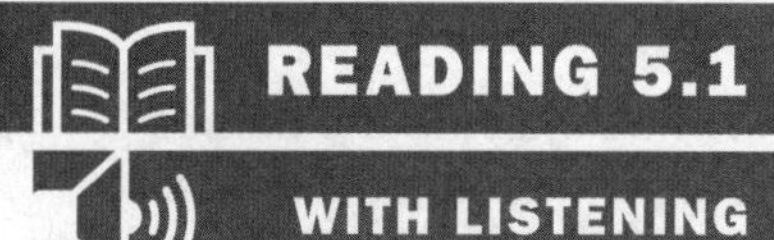

GESTURES AND GIFT-GIVING RULES DIFFER AROUND THE WORLD. Read about some rules that are common in Asia.

GRAMMAR LINK

As you read, you will see some verb choices in parentheses. Underline the correct verb forms. In My eLab, you can listen to this essay and check your answers. While you are listening, pay attention to the speaker's intonation and pronunciation.

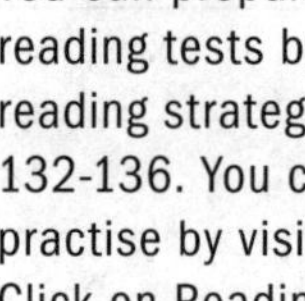

You can prepare for your reading tests by trying the reading strategies on pages 132-136. You can also practise by visiting My eLab. Click on Reading Strategies to find a variety of exercises.

Giving Gifts in Asia

BY C. WINLAND

1 I am a business traveller, and I visit nations around the world. I discovered that every nation has particular gift-giving rules.

2 One of the most interesting nations is Singapore. The government has very effective anti-corruption legislation and prides itself on being one of the most corruption-free countries in the world. In Singapore, government employees cannot accept gifts. The police (will arrest / will arresting) public officials, including government ministers, who accept a bribe.

3 In Singapore, if you want to thank somebody in an office, you (must give / must to give) a gift to everyone. During a 2009 business trip, I wanted to thank a receptionist for her help and hospitality. I (have to gave / had to give) a gift to the entire department. The group graciously accepted my gift.

4 To be polite, most individuals in Singapore and Malaysia will initially refuse a gift. If you continue to insist, the recipients will accept the gift. However, they (won't unwrap / won't unwrapping) it in front of you because it implies that they are impatient and greedy. Instead, they will thank you and then wait to open the gift in private.

5 You also have to consider the type of gift you give. In Singapore and Malaysia, never give a gift that is sharp or that cuts because it symbolizes cutting the relationship. So you (shouldn't buy / shouldn't to buy) a set of knives for your hostess. In Muslim countries, or when you visit a family of practising Muslims, do not bring wine to a meal. The Koran forbids alcohol, so it's a good idea to assume that your hosts (don't drink / doesn't drink). You should even avoid gifts that contain alcohol, such as perfume. In China, you (must not to give / must not give) gifts that are in white or green wrapping paper because those colours are unlucky. In Japan, the number four sounds like the word meaning "death," so most people (won't giving / won't give) gifts that contain four items.

6 Finally, in Japan, if someone (give / gives) you a business card, treat his or her gesture with respect. It is rude to put the card in your pocket immediately. Instead, take the time to read the card. With a nod, acknowledge that you read it. Then you (can put / can putting) it in your pocket.

7 To avoid insulting their hosts, business travellers need to know about gift-giving customs in other nations.

(403 words)

Sources:

"Cultural Competence for Professional Travel in Singapore." *Illinois International*. Illinois International, n.d. Web.

"Singapore Gift Giving Customs." *Giftypedia*. N.p., 29 Oct. 2009. Web.

COMPREHENSION

VOCABULARY

1 In paragraph 2, what is a *bribe*? ______________________

____

2 In paragraph 4, what is the meaning of *unwrap*? (Circle the letter of the correct answer.)

a. Open a gift (remove packaging) b. Accept a gift c. Look at

3 Find a word in paragraph 5 that means "prohibits; does not permit."

____

4 Find a word in paragraph 6 that means "not polite." ______________________

MAIN AND SUPPORTING IDEAS

5 You presented a gift to a business associate in Singapore. He refused to accept the gift three times. What should you do?

a. Keep insisting. He may take it the fourth time.

b. Apologize for offering the gift, and then take it home.

c. Show understanding and offer the gift to his secretary instead. She will open it.

6 You bought this gift for your hostess in Japan. Now she is offended. What mistake did you make?

a. The word for four sounds like "death" in Japanese, and you brought four flowers.

b. Flowers are from the soil and are insulting in Japan.

c. In Japanese, a flower means "love," and your hostess is married.

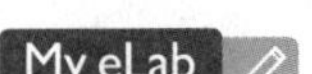

Answer additional questions for all the reading and listening activities in My eLab. You can also access audio and video clips online.

7 You are in Saudi Arabia on an important business trip. You bought a bottle of very old Scotch for the host and perfume for the hostess. The gifts are not wrapped, but they are in their original boxes. Why do your hosts look uncomfortable?

a. Gifts containing alcohol, even perfume, are not appropriate in Muslim countries.

b. Your gifts are considered a bribe, so you insulted your hosts.

c. You did not wrap the gifts. Unwrapped gifts suggest that you have no respect for the hosts.

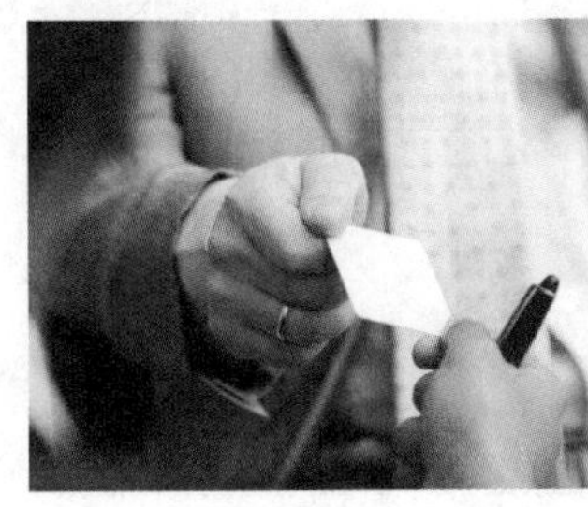

8 You are in Japan, and this man is offering you a business card. What should you do?

a. Examine the card carefully to show that you are reading it. Then put it in your pocket.

b. Politely refuse to accept the card.

c. Immediately put the card in your wallet.

9 What is the principal idea of this essay? ______________________

____

____

WATCHING 5.1 Gringo Trails

Are backpackers destroying the world or saving it? *Gringo Trails* examines the impact of tourism on cultures. Watch the video and answer the following questions.

COMPREHENSION

1 Watch the video and fill in the six missing words.

When I was ________________, I fell in love with travelling. ____________ countries later, I realized my greatest souvenirs were the ______________ I brought back. Later on, when I became a cultural anthropologist, I decided to ____________ a nomadic tribe whose stories I had come to know very well: ____________________. What is our impact? And what are the trails we leave ____________?

2 In what year did Costas Christ visit a beautiful beach in Thailand? ________

3 He told a . . . couple about the beach.

a. French b. German c. Irish d. Spanish

4 What happened to Haad Rin Beach? List five things that changed after Costas Christ's first visit.

____

____

____

____

____

5 What are some messages the video conveys?

____

____

____

DISCUSSION AND WRITING

Create five rules for backpacker tourists.

____

____

____

____

____

READING 5.2

WHEN YOU TRAVEL, MOVEMENTS AND GESTURES CAN HAVE UNINTENDED MEANINGS. Read about some not-so-innocent gestures.

My eLab

You can prepare for your reading tests by trying the reading strategies on pages 132-136. You can also practise by visiting My eLab. Click on Reading Strategies to find a variety of exercises.

Body Language around the Globe

BY VIGO ULLMAN

1 You may assume that gestures and expressions are the same all over the world. A smile is universal, but hand or foot movements can mean entirely different things in other countries.

2 First, when you travel, be careful with your head movements. While most people in the world nod their heads up and down to indicate "yes," in Turkey and Greece an upward nod means "no." A head movement to the side means "yes" in that region of the world. This subtle difference can be rather confusing for tourists.

3 India has a particular head movement that is not common elsewhere: the head wobble. When people tilt their heads from side to side, the meaning depends on the context. If you want to sit in an empty space on a bus, that wobble means "yes, go ahead." If you want to meet someone later, that movement indicates that the person understands. Sometimes it means "maybe" or even "I do not agree with you, but I want to please you." The head shake can also indicate "thanks."

4 Furthermore, eye movements can mean different things around the world. In North America, people can wink to indicate that they like someone. Winking also demonstrates that someone is joking. In Russia, if you wink at a woman, it means that you are calling her a prostitute. In China, a wink can also be offensive.

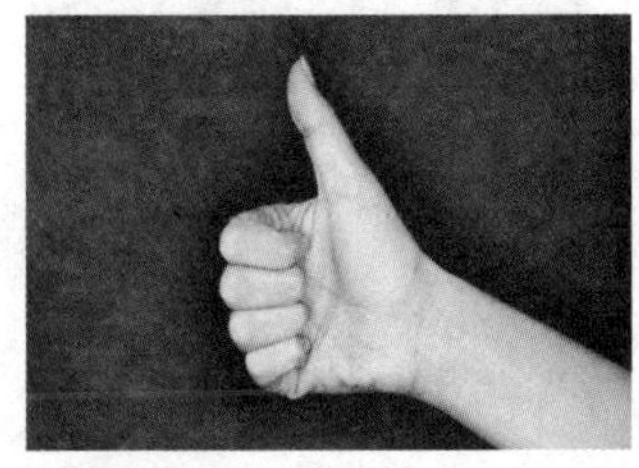

5 Be especially careful with hand gestures. In North America, "thumbs up" has a positive meaning, indicating that you are congratulating someone. It's also used by hitchhikers to ask for a ride. But in Russia and many West African countries, that gesture is a vile insult, meaning "up yours!"

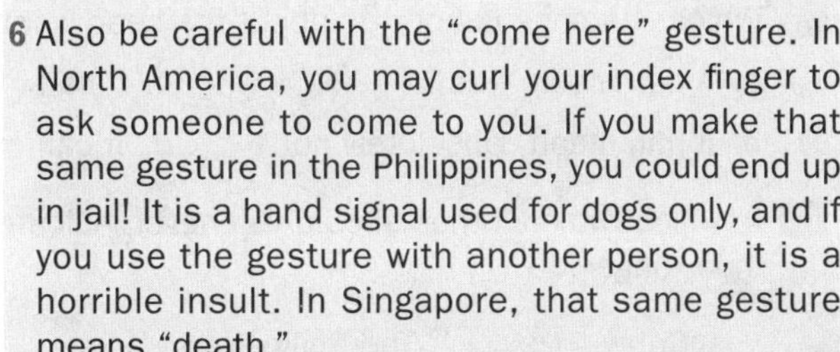

6 Also be careful with the "come here" gesture. In North America, you may curl your index finger to ask someone to come to you. If you make that same gesture in the Philippines, you could end up in jail! It is a hand signal used for dogs only, and if you use the gesture with another person, it is a horrible insult. In Singapore, that same gesture means "death."

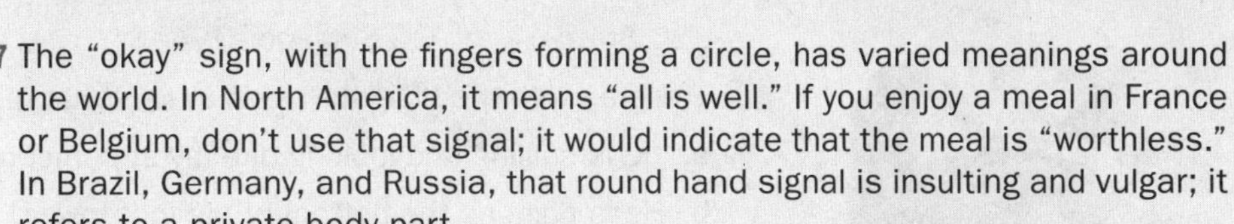

7 The "okay" sign, with the fingers forming a circle, has varied meanings around the world. In North America, it means "all is well." If you enjoy a meal in France or Belgium, don't use that signal; it would indicate that the meal is "worthless." In Brazil, Germany, and Russia, that round hand signal is insulting and vulgar; it refers to a private body part.

8 When you want to acknowledge someone who is across the street, you probably hold up your hand to wave, with your fingers slightly spread. When you want someone to stop, you hold your hand up, palm out. But in Greece, if you show your five fingers like that, you will curse a person's family for five generations. It also means "go to hell."

9 When you travel in Asia or the Middle East, avoid pointing the soles of your feet at other people. Once, while I was travelling in a train from Delhi to Agra, I crossed my legs. The man across from me angrily lectured me and said that I should

never show the sole of my shoe to someone. The gesture meant that I consider the person to be lower than the bottom of my foot. After that, I was careful to keep my feet on the floor! Also remember that in most of the Arab world, people view shoes as dirty. Always remove your shoes when you enter someone's home. In that part of the world, one of the worst insults is to throw your shoe at someone.

10 In many Asian countries, the head, which is the highest part of the body, is considered sacred. Thus, you should never pat a child on the head because your gesture is insulting.

11 Many other gestures can be misinterpreted. If you are planning to travel extensively, take the time to learn about gestures in other countries.

(664 words)

COMPREHENSION

VOCABULARY

1 In paragraph 2, what does *nod* mean?

a. incline b. close c. neck

2 In paragraph 3, what does *wobble* mean?

a. remove b. speak c. move from side to side

3 Find a verb in paragraph 4 that means "closed and opened one eye quickly." (See the photo.)

____

4 In paragraph 8, what does *curse* mean?

a. Say a bad word c. Write

b. Wish to invoke bad fortune on someone

MAIN AND SUPPORTING IDEAS

5 Which sentence is not true about the head wobble in India?

a. It can mean "yes." c. It can mean "I understand."

b. It can mean "absolutely not." d. It can mean "maybe."

6 In which two countries should you never indicate "come here" with a curled index finger?

___ Cuba ___ The Philippines ___ France

___ Brazil ___ Singapore

7 The man with the blue shirt is in India. What mistake is he making?

a. He is smiling and looking directly at someone.

b. He is pointing the bottom of his foot toward someone.

c. He is dressed too formally, so he appears pretentious.

8 In some Asian countries, why should you never pat a child on the head?

____

____

9 What is the principal idea of this essay? In one sentence, explain the main idea. ______________________________

____

____

VOCABULARY **BOOST**

Travel Terms

Do not confuse some travel-related terms.

Travel is generally used as a verb. You **travel** to another place.

Trip is a noun. You take a **trip** somewhere.

noun verb
I took a **trip** to Italy. I **travelled** to Italy.

PRACTICE

Practise using more travel words. Write the letters of the best definitions in the spaces provided.

Terms		Definitions
1. round-trip ticket	_____	a. enter; get on
2. vacancy	_____	b. holiday
3. vacation	_____	c. ticket to a destination and back home
4. book (a ticket)	_____	d. dividing line between two countries
5. border	_____	e. available space in a hotel or motel
6. board (a plane)	_____	f. reserve

SPEAKING Travel Experiences

Work with a partner. To complete each of the following questions, choose the correct word from the list below. Use each word only once. Then ask your partner the questions. Write your partner's answers on the lines.

did do should were will

Partner's name: ______________________________

1 What ________ you do every year during your summer vacation?

____

____

2 Where ________ you travel when you were a child?

____

____

3 What two places ________ your favourite destinations when you were a child?

____

____

4 In the future, where ________ you travel? Explain why.

____

____

5 What ________ people bring with them when they travel? List at least five things.

____

____

WRITING

Write a paragraph about your partner. Include your partner's answers to the questions.

LISTENING PRACTICE

1. Listen to Travel Plans

Listen to Reena's travel plans. Answer the following questions.

1 First name: Reena Last name: ________________

2 Age: ________________

3 Duration of her trip (Choose one answer.)

a. Two weeks b. Two months c. Six months

4 Departure date: ________________

5 Airline for her trip to Beijing: ________________

6 Cost of flight to Beijing: ________________

7 Length of flight to Beijing: ________________

8 Departure time: ________________

9 Arrival time: ________________

10 What countries will she visit? Number the destinations in the correct order.

______ India ______ Thailand ______ China

______ South Korea ______ Singapore ______ Malaysia

2. Follow Directions

Josh Holton is in the city of Glasgow, Scotland. Today he is visiting the city. Follow his journey. Begin on the Start circle. Then follow his path on the map, and write the following places on the map.

bakery   bank   barber   cinema   gallery   hospital

Before you listen, review the following vocabulary.

- **block:** a rectangular section of a city enclosed by streets; the area between two streets
- **turn right** ↱
- **straight ahead** ↑
- **go back**
- **turn left** ↰

LISTENING Travel Tips

Jeremy Stein travels extensively. Listen as he provides some advice for young travellers.

COMPREHENSION

1 How many countries did Stein visit? ____________________

2 How does Stein pay for his trips? ____________________

3 Explain some of Jeremy's travel tips.

Accommodations: ____________________

Luggage: ____________________

Money: ____________________

Phone: ____________________

4 In Jeremy's opinion, should you buy health insurance?

☐ Yes ☐ No

5 What is *haggling*?

a. going back and forth while negotiating a final price

b. eating with your fingers

c. taking an item without paying for it

d. buying cheap items

6 Where does Jeremy plan to go on his next trip? ____________________

7 Where is Stein's family? ____________________

8 How old is Stein? ____________________

READING 5.3

READING CHALLENGE

IN THE NEXT ESSAY, Eileithyia Marshall describes her last family vacation.

PRE-READING VOCABULARY

Before you read, make sure that you understand the following terms.

bird fish fog sand waves

1 ____________________

2 ____________________

3 ____________________

4 ____________________

5 ____________________

My eLab

You can prepare for your reading tests by trying the reading strategies on pages 132-136. You can also practise by visiting My eLab. Click on Reading Strategies to find a variety of exercises.

Laughing through the Fog

BY EILEITHYIA MARSHALL

1 Coastal California exists in stark contrast to all the stereotypes I expected from the "Golden State." As a native of Eastern Canada, my mental image of the West was sunshine, pale sand, and pearly teeth. The home we rented for our trip was advertised as a "beach front oasis" with "striking vistas." As my father drove along State Route 1, I sat in the backseat, imagining piña coladas and blonde boys with surfboards. Our destination was a secluded town called Bodega Bay.

2 The drive from San Francisco was punishing. Next to me sat my younger brother Jack and his friend Henry, who was joining us on our family vacation. I endured two hours of giggling pre-teen boys. When our cramped sedan rolled cautiously through the streets of Bodega Bay, the sky was dim and grey. What was this? I was promised sunbeams and beach bums, not fog and fish odours. We parked and stood outside the rental home.

3 The neighbourhood was silent but for the distant ocean waves—and the birds. Actually, we didn't even notice them right away. It was not until dinner that evening, as the five of us looked out our dining room window, that Jack spoke up: "Did you guys notice that there's a ton of birds out here?"

4 It was true. Birds were everywhere. Gulls, crows, ravens—there were hundreds of them, even thousands. It therefore came as almost no surprise when a quick Google search revealed that Bodega Bay was the real-life setting for Alfred Hitchcock's movie *The Birds*. There are *Birds*-themed landmarks and a *Birds* visitor's centre. On the official town website, they list Nicholas Green, a small child who was tragically murdered, as the most notable resident. It was as if the town picked the theme of "**unsettling**" and ran with it. I was thrilled.

unsettling: perturbing and strange

5 Jack and Henry didn't care about an old black and white movie, and insisted that I accompany them to the beach. The rental house was supposed to be "walking distance to the shore." Hah! It was physically possible to stomp through several miles of weeds to reach the shore, but not without a great deal of complaining from all parties—especially from me. As soon as we reached the sand, Henry sprinted toward the water. To my left, I noticed a warning in massive red and white block letters: DANGER – RIP CURRENTS – DO NOT SWIM!

6 "Henry!" I called, "Get out of the water!" In gleeful and deliberate disregard for my teenaged authority, Henry simply grinned at me and splashed in the water. He knew I could not swim. I was becoming increasingly frantic.

7 Henry paddled farther out. My brother spoke up: "Hey man, there's a riptide! Seriously, come on!" For ten minutes, as I alternated between **coaxing**, pleading, and **swearing**, I wondered how I was going to explain this to the authorities. At last, Henry came skipping back to shore. Later, he admitted that the rip current almost pulled him out. But really, who could have predicted that?

coaxing: persuading

swearing: using vulgar language

8 The trip's highlight was a fishing trip. My father hired an old man to take us out on his boat. It was still dark as we waddled along the dock. Peeking sleepily from above my scarf, I could tell that our Captain was sick of us before we even left land. He fired up the engine and blasted us out to sea. Gravol be damned, I leaned over the edge of the boat and vomited into

the Pacific. When we stopped to cast our lines, we reeled in fish. The actual act of "fishing" required such minimal skill that we felt increasingly guilty as the buckets filled up with rockfish. When we headed back to shore, the world was just waking up, but I was already exhausted.

faded: slowly disappeared

9 Our trip to Bodega Bay could have easily **faded** from our minds—a memory that softens at the edges like an old black and white movie. But those two weeks in August ended up being the last trip we ever took as a family. I soon moved out of my parents' home. Then my mother followed, and my parents split. The family unit dissolved without warning, and I was left trying to preserve the memories I had almost dismissed as "forgettable."

longing: wishing

10 In the ensuing years, I remembered that trip, and it occurred to me that we had, as a family, long existed in our own thick fog. Why we ignored our own chronic unhappiness, I will never fully understand. I think of the moments I simply "endured," and I find myself **longing** for another day, even minute, of that precious, vaguely ominous family time.

(765 words)

COMPREHENSION

GENERAL UNDERSTANDING

1 Why did the family go to Bodega Bay? ______

2 What is Jack's relationship with the writer? ______

3 Why was the writer initially disappointed with Bodega Bay? ______

______

4 What is Bodega Bay famous for? ______

______

5 What happened during the trip? ______

______

6 Why did the writer become worried about Henry? ______

______

7 At the end of the essay, why does the writer feel melancholic? ______

______

______

______

DEFINITIONS AND QUESTIONS

8 Identify six difficult words from the text. Choose words that are not defined above. List the words on a separate piece of paper. Write a definition or description beside each word.

9 On a separate piece of paper, write nine questions for the author. Write three questions about the present, three about the past, and three about the future. You do not have to write the answers to the questions.

WATCHING 5.2 Rip Currents

In Reading 5.3, "Laughing through the Fog," Eileithyia Marshall describes a dangerous rip current. Watch a video showing how to survive the dangerous currents.

COMPREHENSION

1 What is a rip current? ______________________________

____

2 In the two days that preceded the news report, how many rescues were there in Central and South Florida? ______________________________

3 In the US, how many people drown in rip currents every year? ____________

____

4 Give three rules people should follow if they are caught in a rip current. Use *should* or *should not* in each rule.

____

____

____

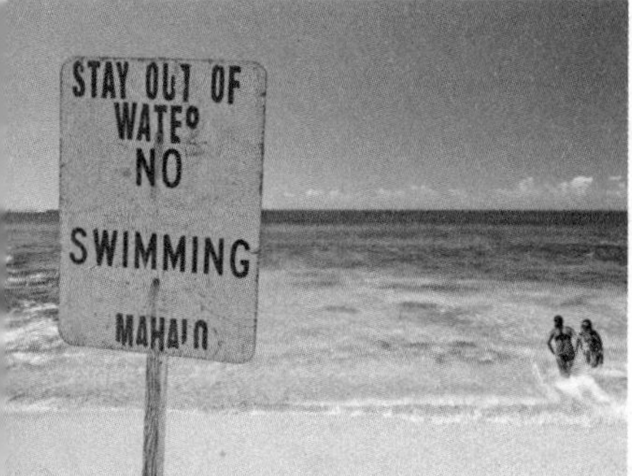

TAKE ACTION!

WRITING TOPICS

Write about one of the following topics. For information about essay structure, see Writing Workshop 2 on pages 141-147.

1 A family Holiday

Write about a vacation that your family took. Use the past tense, and describe where you went and what you did. Who was with you?

2 Travelling

Write an essay about travelling.

- First, explain why people travel. What can they learn when they visit other places?
- Then describe a trip that you took when you were younger. Where did you go? What did you do?
- Finally, describe a place you would like to visit in the future. Explain why you would like to go there.

3 Holidays and Traditions

Write about holidays and traditions.

- First, explain why people in all cultures have special holidays and traditions.
- Then describe a past holiday or celebration that you enjoyed. What happened?
- What will you celebrate in the future? What will you do?

SPEAKING TOPICS

1 Local Tourism

Make a video or a PowerPoint presentation. Choose one of the following topics. Your audience is people from other countries.

a. Describe a cultural holiday or celebration that is popular in your region. How do people prepare for the event?

b. Promote your town or city to tourists. Explain why people should visit it. What can they do? Discuss specific attractions in your area.

c. Describe a certain type of cuisine that is popular in your region. Explain how to make the food or describe the best place to find the food.

d. Give advice for visitors who are coming to your area. What should they pack? What is the weather like? What information do travellers need if they are coming to your region?

e. Describe a traditional, unusual, or new sport or game that is popular in your region. Briefly give important features of the sport. Remember that your audience is not familiar with the sport.

2 Travel Project

Talk about a place that you visited or you would like to visit. Present some basic information about that place. Your presentation should include most of the following information.

- Location: Explain where the place is located.
- Cost: What is the best price for plane tickets to that location?
- Currency: What kind of currency will people need? What is the exchange rate?
- Accommodations: Where can a student stay? Do some research online to find inexpensive accommodations.
- Attractions: Describe some things that visitors can do in that place.

My eLab

To practise vocabulary from this chapter, visit My eLab.

SPEAKING PRESENTATION TIPS

- **Practise your presentation and time yourself.** You should speak for about two minutes (or for a length of time determined by your teacher).
- **Use cue cards.** Do not read! Put about fifteen keywords on your cue cards.
- **Bring visual support,** such as a picture, photograph, object, video, or PowerPoint slides.
- **Classmates will ask you questions about your presentation.** You must also ask your classmates about their presentations. Review how to form questions before your presentation day.

REVISING AND EDITING

REVISE FOR AN INTRODUCTION AND EDIT FOR MODALS

A piece of writing should begin with an introduction. (To learn more about introductions, see Writing Workshop 2 on pages 141-147.)

Read the short essay and follow these steps.

1 Underline and correct five verb or modal errors, not including the example.

2 Write a short introduction. It can consist of three or four sentences. End your introduction with a thesis statement. The thesis expresses the main focus of the essay.

Travel Tips

Introduction: ____

____

____

____

____

____

First, carefully plan what you will <u>bringing</u> [bring]. You should not packing too many clothes. You will want to buy souvenirs, so leave some extra space in your bag. Pack some medical supplies, such as bandages. Also, you should to bring a very comfortable pair of shoes.

Before you travel somewhere, learn about the country's requirements. Canadians must shows a passport before they enter the United States. Many countries also demand a visa. For example, China wo'nt let you enter the country unless you have a tourist visa.

So remember to pack the necessities. Also, learn about visa and passport requirements. If you prepare for your trip, you should having a great vacation.

GRAMMAR TIP

Using *Will*

For the future tense, use the same form of the verb with every subject. Use *will* + the base form of the verb. The negative form of *will* is *will not* or *won't*.

He **will** ~~travels~~ [travel] with his wife. He **won't** buy too many presents.

To learn more about the future tense, see Unit 6 in *Avenues 1: English Grammar*.

CHAPTER 6

RISK-TAKING AND SURVIVAL

"Take calculated risks. That is quite different from being rash."

— GEORGE S. PATTON (US ARMY GENERAL)

Are you a thrill seeker? Do you like adventure sports? In this chapter, you will read about survival and risk-taking.

Extreme Sports

Risky Activities

Work with a small group. Take turns chatting about the following topics. You can change topics at any time. When the teacher flicks the lights on and off, change speakers.

1. Which of the activities below is the safest? Explain why.
2. Which activity is the most dangerous? Explain why.
3. Which activities would you like to try? Explain why.

surfing

skydiving

BMX biking

rafting

Compare Sports

Work with a partner, and compare the people and activities in the photos above. On a separate sheet of paper, write five sentences. Your sentences should include the following words. If you need help forming your sentences, refer to the Grammar Tip below.

crazier easiest harder fastest most expensive

GRAMMAR
TIP

Making Comparisons

Use comparative forms when you compare two people or things.

In general, when adjectives have only one syllable, add *-er* to form the comparative and *-est* to form the superlative.

Skateboards are small**er** than surfboards.

Kara is the young**est** person in my family.

When adjectives have two or more syllables, add *more* to form the comparative and *most* to form the superlative.

Mountain climbing is **more dangerous** than cycling.

Mountain climbing is **the most dangerous** activity.

To learn more about comparative forms, see Unit 10 in *Avenues 1: English Grammar.*

READING 6.1

LEARN ABOUT SOME ACTIVITIES THAT BOOST ADRENALINE. Read about each activity, and indicate if you would do it or not. Explain why. Use your dictionary, if needed.

Adrenaline Adventures

lurked: hid and waited

1 Prehistoric humans didn't need to chase hurricanes or go bungee jumping. Their daily quest for survival—in an age where danger **lurked** around every rock—provided them with all the adrenaline they needed. In contrast, modern life is much safer, but it's also decidedly duller, which is why the demand for adventure holidays and extreme sports is booming. People need to feel alive again, and that occurs when they flirt with danger. There are plenty of adrenaline activities to choose from.

1219 metres: 4000 feet

4 metres: 13 feet

2 **Skywalk, China** Known locally as the "walk of faith," this vertigo-inducing pathway is bolted to the side of Tianmen Mountain in Hunan, China. Perched some **1219 metres** above a rocky ravine, the path is made of glass and has fantastic views of the canyon below. This skywalk is about **4 metres** longer than a similar structure, the Grand Canyon skywalk in Arizona.

Would you do this activity? ☐ Yes ☐ No

Explain why: ______________________________

____

My eLab

You can prepare for your reading tests by trying the reading strategies on pages 132-136. You can also practise by visiting My eLab. Click on Reading Strategies to find a variety of exercises.

3 **Storm Chasing, USA** Tornadoes are frequent in "Tornado Alley." Most residents living in that tornado zone flee their homes at the first sign of extreme weather. While local residents are moving to a safer place, adrenaline junkies chase the storm. Driving in cars, trucks, and vans, storm chasers are fascinated by the dangerous power of Mother Nature. Typically, storm-chasing tours last six days and follow tornadoes as they whip up chaos across Texas, Oklahoma, Kansas, and Nebraska. Some companies guarantee a storm or you get your money back.

Would you do this activity? ☐ Yes ☐ No

Explain why: ______________________________

____

3500-kilometre: 2175-mile

4 **Rickshaw Run, India** This epic **3500-kilometre** rally is on some of the most extreme roads in India. But, rather than using 4x4s, participants in the Rickshaw Run cram into auto-rickshaws, which have about as much power as a hairdryer. The website for the attraction calls the rickshaws "glorified lawn mowers." There is no set route, no support crew, and no guarantee you'll make it to the end. Still, it's a lot of fun, and all proceeds go to the Cool Earth charity, which aims to stop deforestation.

Would you do this activity? ☐ Yes ☐ No

Explain why: ____

____

5 EdgeWalk, Canada Live life on the edge at the CN Tower in Toronto. The **609-metre** communications tower provides the world's highest hands-free observation experience. Participants are attached to a harness via an overhead rail, which prevents them from falling onto the street below. According to the EdgeWalk website, "Trained EdgeWalk guides will encourage participants to push their personal limits, allowing them to lean back over Toronto with nothing but air and breathtaking views of Lake Ontario beneath them."

609-metre: 1997-foot

Would you do this activity? ☐ Yes ☐ No

Explain why: ____

____

6 Cage of Death, Australia Flirt with the jaws of Australia's most feared reptile at Crocosaurus Cove in Darwin, home to the infamous Cage of Death. There's room for two in the glass cage, which is lowered into an aquarium containing some rather lively saltwater crocs. Visitors spend fifteen minutes in the cage, where they can watch the large creatures swim around the enclosure and possibly ram into it.

Would you do this activity? ☐ Yes ☐ No

Explain why: ____

____

7 Running with the Bulls, Spain Every July, the narrow cobblestone streets of Pamplona fill with charging bulls. Running with the bulls, which began hundreds of years ago, was originally a way to move bulls from fields outside the city, down narrow roads, to the bullring. Locals would chase the bulls with sticks. Today, international tourists run, terrified, as the dangerous half-ton beasts pound the pavement behind them. Behind fences, spectators watch the action. From 1924, when records were first kept, to 2009, fourteen people died doing the activity. *Time* journalist Randy James says, "Another factor fueling injuries in Pamplona is alcohol." Participants are not supposed to run if they are tipsy, but many break the rules and drink before running.

Would you do this activity? ☐ Yes ☐ No

Explain why: ____

____

15,200 metres: 50,000 feet

8 **Space Flight, USA** Virgin Galactic is offering the trip of a lifetime with short flights just above the earth's atmosphere. Passengers will experience the sensation of weightlessness. The fleet of suborbital spacecraft will reach altitudes of **15,200 metres**. The suborbital trip will take off from New Mexico. However, the project was delayed after a 2014 accident, when SpaceShip Two broke apart in midair and debris fell into a California desert. Virgin Galactic owner Richard Branson remains optimistic that ordinary people will experience space flights. Tickets, which start at $250,000, are beyond most people's budgets, but the company already has a waiting list of potential passengers.

Would you do this activity? ☐ Yes ☐ No

Explain why: ______________________________

____

(685 words)

Sources:

Paragraphs 1-6, 8: McPhillips, Candace. "Getting High: Fifteen of the Best Adrenaline Activities." *World Travel Guide*. Columbus Travel Media, n.d. Web. © Originally published on World Travel Guide (www.worldtravelguide.net).

Paragraph 7: James, Randy. "A Brief History of the Running of the Bulls." *Time*. Time Inc., 07 Jul. 2009. Web.

COMPREHENSION

TEAM ANALYSIS

Work with a partner or team. Discuss your answers and write your team's opinion.

1. Which are the two safest activities?

______________ ______________

Why are they safer than the other activities? ______________

____

2 Which are the two most dangerous activities?

______________ ______________

Why are they more dangerous than the other activities? ______________

____

3 What are the risks involved in those activities? Write at least three risks.

____

____

4 What benefits do people get from doing adrenaline activities? Think of two or three benefits. ______________

____

____

VOCABULARY

5 Find a word in paragraph 1 that means "more boring." ______________

6 Find a word in paragraph 2 that means "attached with metal fasteners." ____________

7 Find a word in paragraph 3 that means "escape from; run away from." ____________

8. Find a word in paragraph 6 that means "hit with force." ____________

9 Find a word in paragraph 7 that is the opposite of *wide*. ____________

10 Find a word in paragraph 7 that means "slightly inebriated; a little drunk." ____________

My eLab

Answer additional reading and listening questions in My eLab. You can also access audio and video clips online.

VOCABULARY BOOST

Make, Do, Play, and *Go*

Make means "construct, manufacture, or create."

Make a cake, a sculpture, a decision, lunch, a meal, a promise

Do means "perform or accomplish." Also, you do an athletic activity.

Do exercise, gymnastics, aerobics, Tai Chi

Also **do** homework, housework, the dishes, the cleaning, the ironing

Play means "participate in a game or sport." You also play an instrument.

Play soccer, baseball, hockey, chess, the piano, the violin

Go + *verb* (*-ing* form) refers to a physical activity that you do alone.

Go running, skiing, swimming, snowboarding*

* Note: You can also use just the action verb: I run, ski, swim, snowboard.

PRACTICE

Fill in the blanks with the correct verb: *make, do, play,* or *go*.

1 I am very busy. I ________ physical activities every day. On Mondays, I ________ jogging. Every Tuesday, I ____________ soccer or I ____________ hockey. In the summer I ________ hiking, and in the winter I ________ skiing. I sometimes ________ Tai Chi to relax. I also ____________ tennis when I find the time. Do you ____________ football or baseball?

2 I live alone, so I ________ the cooking and cleaning at home. I ____________ my own meals. I ____________ supper every night. Do you ________ the cleaning? What activities do you ________ ?

My eLab

For more practice using *make, do, play,* and *go*, visit My eLab.

WATCHING 6.1 Extreme Climber

Alex Honnold is an extreme climber. Watch the ABC news report about Honnold's adventures.

COMPREHENSION

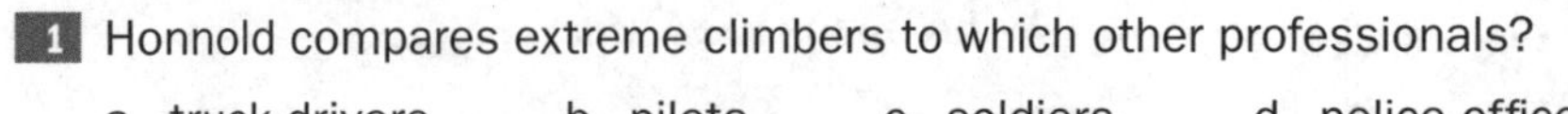

1 Honnold compares extreme climbers to which other professionals?

a. truck drivers b. pilots c. soldiers d. police officers

2 When the video was made, how old was Honnold? ____________________

3 Why does Cedar Wright worry about Honnold? ____________________

____

4 What is free-soloing? ____________________

5 Does Honnold sometimes stop a climb if it doesn't feel right?

☐ Yes ☐ No

6 Which bank made a TV commercial that featured Honnold?

a. the bank of Montreal b. Citibank c. the National Bank

7 How does Honnold live? Describe his lifestyle. ____________________

____

8 Why did the company Clif Bar stop endorsing extreme climbers?

a. The company was losing money.

b. The company had a fight with Honnold.

c. The company felt that the climbers took too many extreme risks.

9 What was Honnold afraid of in the past?

a. speaking in public b. flying c. being in the dark

DISCUSSION

What is your opinion of climbers like Honnold?

SPEAKING Sports

Work with a partner. Ask your partner the following questions. Write your partner's answers on the lines provided.

Partner's name: ____________________

1 When you were a child, what sports did you play? ____________________

____

2 What is your favourite sport? Explain why. ____________________

____

3 Do you prefer to do solo or team sports? Explain why. ____________________

____

4 What are the most important sports and games in your region? Rank the top three sports in order of their popularity.

____________________ ____________________ ____________________

5 What are two of the most dangerous team sports? Explain why they are dangerous.

1. ____________________

2. ____________________

6 Why do people in every culture enjoy sports and games? Think of at least two reasons. ____________________

____

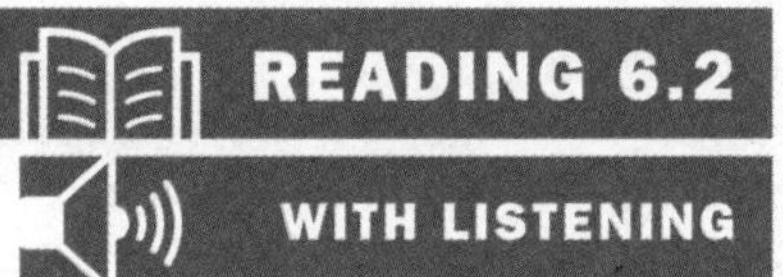

BMX—BICYCLE MOTOCROSS—IS A POPULAR SPORT. Kara Bruce discovered BMX riding when she was twenty-one. In this interview, she discusses why she does this risky sport.

GRAMMAR LINK

As you read, you will see some word choices in parentheses. Underline the correct word(s). In My eLab, you can listen to this essay and check your answers. While you are listening, pay attention to the speaker's intonation and pronunciation.

BMX Rider: Interview with Kara Bruce

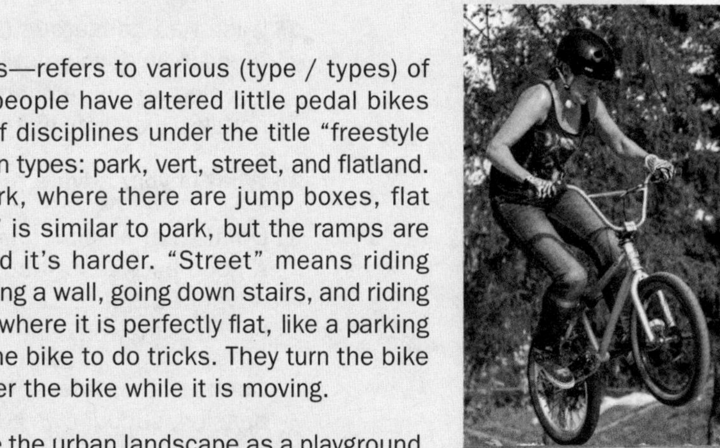

1 **Kara, what is BMX?**

2 BMX—Bicycle Motocross—refers to various (type / types) of biking. Over the years, people have altered little pedal bikes and created a new set of disciplines under the title "freestyle BMX." There are four main types: park, vert, street, and flatland. "Park" means skate park, where there are jump boxes, flat banks, and so on. "Vert" is similar to park, but the ramps are (more high / higher) and it's harder. "Street" means riding around the street and riding a wall, going down stairs, and riding on a **ledge**. "Flatland" is where it is perfectly flat, like a parking lot. Flatland riders use the bike to do tricks. They turn the bike upside down or climb over the bike while it is moving.

ledge: flat narrow horizontal surface

3 I'm a "street" rider. I use the urban landscape as a playground. I (very / really) love looking at a handrail, bench, or stairs in a new light.

My eLab

You can prepare for your reading tests by trying the reading strategies on pages 132-136. You can also practise by visiting My eLab. Click on Reading Strategies to find a variety of exercises.

4 **How did you get into this sport?**

5 I watched videos and chatted with girls who ride BMX. Nina Buitrago, from the US, was one of the first girls to do freestyle and compete with the guys. Nina has sponsors, so BMX is her life. Because of her, there are now girl events at competitions. So at first, I (taught / thought) that it was a terrifying boy's sport. But after I watched *Ray's Weekend*, which shows girls riding and doing tricks, I realized that I could ride too.

6 Six years ago, my friend Lee gave me a BMX frame, and I bought second-hand parts and built a decent bike. (Than / Then) I bought a better bike and upgraded some parts. At first, I did simple tricks, but with practice I got (better / more better) at this sport.

7 BMX is a great way to meet people. It's not a team sport, so you don't have to show up on a schedule. You can go any time, and everyone is friendly and helpful. I have friends all over the world who I met in parks or online. Last summer, when I did a road trip to the US, I sometimes stayed with online BMX friends. In Florida, a girl let me stay in her place. She had to leave for (a / the) funeral, but she left a key for me. She trusted me because we share this sport. I even contacted Nina Buitrago, and now I consider her a friend.

8 **Do you have a risk-taking personality?**

9 No. I was a (child nervous / nervous child) and was scared of hurting myself. I imagined horrible ways of dying. Now I deal with anxieties in a creative way. BMX helps me to mentally and physically conquer a fear. Riding on a ledge might look easy, but it's scary. This sport is a giant game of body and mind.

10 **Do you hurt yourself sometimes?**

11 I broke my collarbone, wrist, and hand. Recently, I got a deep cut on my chin. My last accident occurred partly because I had a new bike frame, so the geometry was different. A shorter frame has more kick to it. Also, Cory Coffey was there. She is the first girl to do a back flip, so I was a bit intimidated. I over-cleared a jump, and I wiped out.

12 **You weren't focused?**

13 Actually, being too focused isn't good. You need to be chilled out. I ride best when I'm loose and relaxed.

14 **Is this sport too risky?**

15 It isn't as dangerous (as / than) people think. Not all riders get injured. My friend Ryan does amazing double back flips, and he never hurts himself. Anyway, people can injure themselves at the gym. People hurt themselves by doing nothing. Inactivity is a killer.

16 **What is your advice to anyone who wants to try this sport?**

17 Do it! Wear a helmet and mouth guard. Get a decent bike that's not too heavy. A good bike costs about $800, but intro bikes are (more cheap / cheaper). Advanced riders custom-build their own bikes, which can cost thousands because they buy special frames, hubs, tires, pedals, and so on.

18 Contact other riders! There is a worldwide community of BMXers. We share a passion, set our own goals, and put effort into progressing. We help each other learn tricks and push past our fears.

(696 words)

COMPREHENSION

VOCABULARY

1 Identify the parts of a bike. Write the correct word to go with each image.

pedal frame helmet handlebars tires

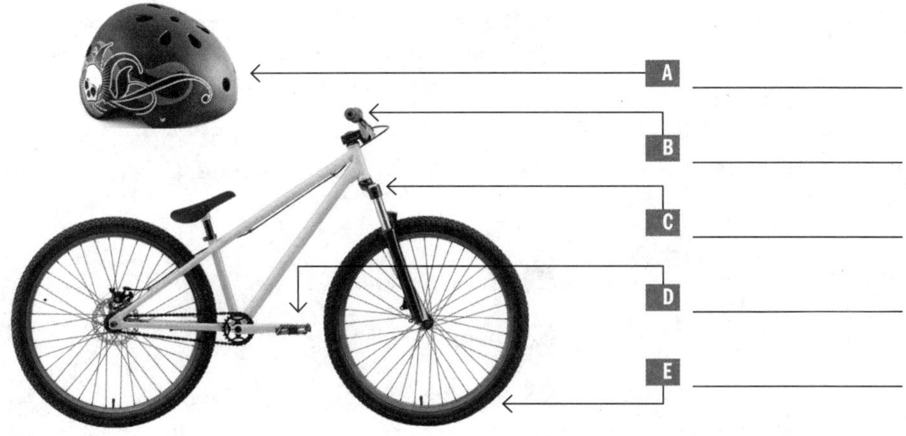

2 In paragraph 2, the opposite of "right side up" is ____________.

3 In paragraph 11, what does *wiped out* mean?

a. fell off my bike b. felt extremely tired c. moved

4 In paragraph 13, what does *chilled out* mean?

a. nervous b. relaxed c. prepared

GENERAL UNDERSTANDING

Circle *T* for "true" or *F* for "false." Write true sentences under any false statements.

5 Kara's favourite type of BMX riding is "street." T F

____

6 BMX is not a team sport, so it is a very lonely sport. T F

____

7 When she was a child, Kara was very anxious T F

____

8 Kara never injured herself doing BMX biking. T F

____

9 When she rides BMX, Kara tries to be very focused. T F

____

10 Kara suggests that new riders buy a decent bike that is not too heavy. T F

____

LISTENING PRACTICE

1. Identify Silent Letters

Repeat each pair of words after the speaker. Then circle the silent sound. You will hear each word twice. (For rules about silent letters, and for other pronunciation tips, see Appendix 4.)

			Silent Sound					Silent Sound	
Example:	listen,	castle	(t)	l					
1	know	knife	k	n	6	hour	honest	h	o
2	thumb	climb	m	b	7	walk	talk	l	k
3	design	sign	g	n	8	plumber	comb	m	b
4	should	could	l	d	9	often	listen	n	t
5	write	wrong	r	w	10	thought	light	gh	t

2. Complete the Sentences

Listen to each sentence and underline the words that you hear. Listen carefully to word endings.

[1]Kate Lund likes to take risks. She knows that she (should / shouldn't). [2]However, she (can / can't) stop herself. She is a risk taker.

[3]Last (Tuesday / Thursday), Kate decided to try car surfing. [4]The 19-(years / year)-old woman was with her boyfriend Matt. [5]Kate decided to (climb / climbing / climbed) onto the roof of the car, and Matt drove. [6]It (was / isn't / wasn't) a good idea. [7]When Matt stopped at a stop (sing / sign), Kate fell off the roof. [8]She hurt (his / her) back, but she survived. [9]These days, she is lucky that she (can / can't) still walk.

[10]The police charged Matt with dangerous driving. He (can / can't) leave the province. [11]He (can / can't) speak with his friends. [12]However, he (can / can't) drive a car. [13]Matt (could / couldn't) lose his license. [14]Kate (should / shouldn't) car surf again! [15]Hopefully, Kate and Matt (can / can't / won't) make the same mistakes in the future.

LISTENING Lost in the Wild

On the CBC program *Wire Tap*, Jonathan Goldstein spoke with Cary J. Griffith, author of *Lost in the Wild*. His book includes the story of Jason Rasmussen, a third-year medical student who made a two-day trek into a remote area of the woods. When he stepped away from his campsite, he made a series of mistakes that left him separated from his supplies. Griffith also discusses three boys who got lost in Gooseberry State Park. Listen to the interview and answer the following questions.

COMPREHENSION

1 What are the first two emotions that people feel when they realize that they are lost? ______

2 How long was Cary Griffith lost in the woods? ______

3 What are Griffith's six basic rules for when you go for a walk in the woods?

1. ______
2. ______
3. ______
4. ______
5. ______
6. ______

READING 6.3 The Rules of Survival

My eLab

You can prepare for your reading tests by trying the reading strategies on pages 132-136. You can also practise by visiting My eLab. Click on Reading Strategies to find a variety of exercises.

Laurence Gonzales is an award-winning writer. The next excerpt is from his book, *Deep Survival*.

The Rules of Survival

BY LAURENCE GONZALES

1 As a journalist, I write about accidents in an effort to understand who lives, who dies, and why. There is a strange uniformity in the way people survive seemingly impossible circumstances. Decades and sometimes centuries apart, separated by culture, geography, and tradition, the most successful survivors go through the same patterns of thought and behaviour. It doesn't seem to matter whether they are surviving being lost in the wilderness or battling cancer; the strategies remain the same. Survival should be thought of as a **journey**. Here are a few things I learned about survival.

journey: trip; voyage

Stay Calm

2 In the initial crisis, survivors are not ruled by fear; instead, they make use of it. Their fear often feels like anger, which motivates them and makes them feel sharper. Hiker Aron Ralston had to cut off his hand to free himself from a stone that was **trapping** him in a Utah canyon. He initially panicked and slammed himself against the boulder. But then he stopped, did some deep breathing, and began thinking about his options. He spent five days progressing through the stages necessary to convince him of the decisive action he had to take to save himself.

trapping: preventing from getting free

Think, Analyze, and Plan

3 Survivors quickly organize, set up routines, and institute discipline. Steve Callahan, a sailor and boat designer, was rammed by a whale, and his boat sank while he was on a solo voyage in 1982. He was **adrift** in the Atlantic for seventy-six days on a small raft. He experienced his survival voyage as taking place

adrift: floating

under the command of a "captain" who gave him his orders and kept him on his water ration, even as his own mutinous (emotional) spirit complained. His interior "captain" routinely lectured "the crew." He was able to push away thoughts that his situation was hopeless and take the necessary first steps of the survival journey: to think clearly, analyze his situation, and formulate a plan.

Celebrate Every Victory

stranded: left alone

4 Survivors take great joy from even their smallest successes. This attitude helps keep motivation high and prevents them from feeling hopeless. Lauren Elder was the only survivor of a light plane crash in the High Sierra. **Stranded** on a 12,000-foot peak, with a broken arm, she could see the San Joaquin Valley below. A vast wilderness and icy cliffs separated her from safety. Wearing a skirt and blouse but no underwear, with high-heeled boots, she crawled "on all fours," as she balanced on the ice crust, punching through it with her hands. She had thirty-six hours of climbing ahead of her, which seemed impossible. Elder focused only as far as the next big rock. After she completed her descent of the first pitch, Elder felt exhilarated: "I gave a whoop that echoed down the silent pass." A good survivor always tells herself, "Count your blessings–you're alive."

Enjoy the Survival Journey

Auschwitz: concentration camp created by the Nazis during World War II

5 Even in the worst circumstances, survivors find some way to play and laugh. Survival can be tedious, and waiting is an art. Elder found herself laughing out loud when she started to worry that someone might see up her skirt as she climbed. In **Auschwitz**, Viktor Frankl's companions were losing hope. He ordered them to think of one funny thing each day. Singing, playing mind games, reciting poetry, and doing mathematical problems can make waiting tolerable.

Never Give Up

6 Yes, you might die. But perhaps it doesn't have to be today. Don't let it worry you. Forget about rescue. Everything you need is inside you already. Dougal Robertson, a sailor who spent thirty-eight days on a small life boat after his schooner sank, advised thinking of survival this way: "Rescue will come as a welcome interruption of ... the survival voyage."

Apollo 13: US space craft that was sent to the moon in 1970

7 Survivors are not easily discouraged by setbacks. They accept that the environment constantly changes. They know that they must adapt. When they fall, they pick themselves up and start the entire process over again. When **Apollo 13**'s oxygen tank exploded, Commander Jim Lovell chose to continue transmitting data back to mission control, even as they burned up on re-entry. Elder and Callahan were equally determined and knew this final truth: If you're still alive, there is always one more thing that you can do.

(695 words)

Source:
Gonzales, Laurence. *Deep Survival: Who Lives, Who Dies, and Why*. New York: W.W. Norton, 2003. Print.

COMPREHENSION

VOCABULARY

1 Find a word in paragraph 1 that means "fighting." ____________

2 Find a word in paragraph 3 that means "a floating platform (not a boat)." ____________

3 In paragraph 3, what is the meaning of *sank*?

a. fell on its side b. ruptured c. submerged below the surface

4 In paragraph 4, what is the meaning of *pitch*?

a. land that inclines b. throw c. high tone of voice

5 Find a word in paragraph 7 that means "defeats or reverses." ____________

SUPPORTING IDEAS

6 The author describes the experiences of several survivors. Briefly explain what challenge the following people faced. The paragraph numbers are in parentheses.

a) Aron Ralston (2): ____________

b) Steve Callahan (3): ____________

c) Lauren Elder (4): ____________

d) Viktor Frankl (5): ____________

e) Dougal Robertson (6): ____________

7 What lessons does this essay provide for the reader? ____________

WATCHING 6.2 Survival Skills

PART 1: How to Survive a Tornado

What should you do if you hear a tornado warning? What are the biggest dangers you face during a tornado? Watch the video and learn how to survive a tornado.

WRITING

In a paragraph, describe the steps that you should take. Include the following information.

- What are the biggest dangers during a tornado?
- If you are outside during a tornado, what should you do?
- If you are in a house during a tornado, what steps should you take?
- After a tornado, if you are trapped by debris, what should you do?

PART 2: How to Survive a Car Crash through Ice

What should you do if you are driving on a lake and your car crashes through the ice? Watch and find out. Then answer the following questions.

WRITING

In a paragraph, describe the steps that you should take. Include the following information.

- How do car companies test cars for cold weather?
- If a car is sinking, should you use your cellphone to call someone?
- What are the four things to remember if your car falls through the ice?
- What should you do if the electricity in your car stops working when it falls through the ice?

READING 6.4

READING CHALLENGE

ARE PARENTS OVERPROTECTIVE THESE DAYS? Read about some unusual parents. As you read, think about your own adolescence. Afterwards, you will respond to the reading.

You can prepare for your reading tests by trying the reading strategies on pages 132-136. You can also practise by visiting My eLab. Click on Reading Strategies to find a variety of exercises.

A Lesson in Brave Parenting

BY BRUCE BARCOTT

1 Abby Sunderland is from Thousand Oaks, California. In 2010, the sixteen-year-old girl embarked on a non-stop sailing trip. Travelling alone, Abby hoped to become the youngest person to sail around the world. She travelled for 12,000 nautical miles. Then on June 10, she was in the Indian Ocean thousands of kilometres west of Australia when large waves broke the mast of her boat. She was able to activate emergency beacons, and authorities realized she was in trouble. Two days later, a French fishing boat rescued the teenager.

2 What in heaven's name were her parents thinking? For a lot of people, that was the second thought that came to mind after hearing of Abby's rescue. The first thought, of course, was "Thank God she's alive."

3 Now that Abby is okay, the inevitable storm of criticism is raining down on her parents, Laurence and Marianne. They wished their daughter bon voyage when she cast off from Marina del Rey in January. They allowed a sixteen-year-old girl to sail alone around the world. Were they insane?

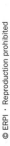

4 Unusual, yes. But they are hardly "the worst parents in the world," as I heard them called recently. In fact, they may be the opposite. In a similar case, thirteen-year-old Jordan Romero climbed Mount Everest. Jordan's father, Paul Romero, and the Sunderlands are practising something rare these days: brave parenting.

5 I have an eleven-year-old and an eight-year-old. Raising kids today is like working on a construction site with an overzealous risk manager. Everywhere there are signs reminding parents that Safety Is Job One. Parents are told to cut up hot dogs and grapes to prevent choking, to place the kids into car seats, and to watch children vigilantly at the park. A certain amount of this is progress, of course. But in our obsession with safety, we are losing sight of the upside of risk, danger, and even injury. We can raise **bold** children who are prepared for adventure and eager to embrace the unfamiliar.

bold: courageous

6 The habitat of my own children is restricted. It contains entirely too many screens and couches. And this constraint is not unique to my family. Sandra Hofferth, a researcher at the University of Maryland, found that the amount of time kids spent outside doing things such as walking, hiking, fishing, and beach play declined by 50 percent between 1997 and 2003. Not long ago, up to half of the kids in this country walked or rode their bikes to school. Now fewer than one in five do. That inactivity has consequences. In the 1960s, fewer than 5 percent of American kids were obese. Now it's close to 20 percent. So seldom do kids **wander** in the woods that "nature deficit disorder" has become a common concern among parents of my generation.

wander: walk with no definite destination

7 The Sunderlands are not crazy. They are subversives. They are acting against a dominant culture that fills parents with fear. Parents blame themselves every time their child **skins** a knee.

skins: damages by stripping the skin from

8 To be clear, brave parenting is not synonymous with wise parenting. I have my own reservations about permitting a thirteen-year-old like Jordan Romero to climb Mount Everest. One veteran Everest climber told me, "I'm not sure a thirteen-year-old can be fully cognizant of the lethality of that environment." To me, the limit in these situations should be age sixteen.

9 While I question the wisdom of permitting a thirteen-year-old to go up a Himalayan peak, I cannot criticize the impulse behind it. I applaud it. Personally, I am not planning to climb Mount Everest with my eleven-year-old daughter. We won't even try Mount Rainier. That's not who she is. And if it were, she would still be too young. But the brave parenting of the Sunderlands and the Romeros forces me to reconsider the constraints I put on my kids. It helps me lead my son and daughter to the edge of the woods and tell them, "Go farther now, on your own."

(661 words)

Source:

Barcott, Bruce. "A Lesson in Brave Parenting." *Los Angeles Times*. Los Angeles Times, 16 June 2010. Web.

COMPREHENSION

GENERAL UNDERSTANDING

1 What did Abby Sunderland hope to do in 2010? ______________________

____

2 When Jordan Romero tried to climb Mount Everest, how old was he?

____

3. What ideas are found in paragraph 5? Put a check mark (✓) beside three supporting points.

___ The writer, Bruce Barcott, has two children.

___ These days, children take too many risks and hurt themselves.

___ Parents are too obsessed with the safety of their children.

___ Risk and danger have positive points: children become more courageous and adventurous.

___ Parents spend too much money on their children.

4. What is the writer's opinion of his own children's environment? See paragraph 6. ____

____

5. What is the writer's opinion of Abby Sunderland's parents?

a. They are crazy and dangerous parents.

b. They are courageous and subversive parents.

c. They are ordinary parents.

6. What is the main message of this text? ____

____

WRITING

Respond to "Brave Parenting." Were Abby Sunderland's parents reckless by letting their daughter do the solo voyage? Should parents let their children take extreme risks?

VOCABULARY BOOST

Let or *Leave*

Let means "permit."

Leave means "go away." It can also mean "forget" or "place in a specific location."

My parents **let** us borrow the car. We cannot **leave** the car on the street.

PRACTICE

Fill in the blanks with *let* or *leave*.

1. My parents are very easygoing. They __________ me stay out late. I have no curfew. But they don't __________ me drink and drive. If I drink, I have to __________ the car behind and take a taxi.

2. Sometimes my parents __________ me have parties. Their only condition is that I clean up afterwards. If I __________ plates or glasses on the floor, my parents will be angry.

My eLab

Practise using *leave*, *let*, and other vocabulary from this chapter.

SPEAKING Parenting Rules

Discuss the following questions with a partner or in small groups.

1 Is it better for parents to be permissive or overprotective? Explain why.

2 From the perspective of a parent, discuss reasonable rules for adolescents. Consider the following issues. Think about youths between thirteen and fifteen years of age.

a) Curfew (an established time to be home at night)

b) Driving

c) Drugs and alcohol

d) Travel (without parents)

3 What should parents do when teenagers break the rules?

WRITING

In a 250-word essay, discuss rules for adolescents.

- First, explain which type of parent is better: a permissive parent or an overprotective one.
- Then describe your childhood and adolescence. What rules did your parents or guardians set? Were they permissive or overprotective? Describe a time when you broke a rule or made a bad decision. What happened?
- Finally, explain what rules you will set for your children. What type of parent will you be?

GRAMMAR TIP

Using *Should*

When you give advice, you can use the modal auxiliary *should* + the base form of the verb.

Never add *-s* or *-ed* to the verb that follows *should*.

watch
A small child should not ~~watches~~ too much television.

To learn more about modal auxiliaries, see Unit 9 in *Avenues 1: English Grammar*.

My eLab

To practise vocabulary from this chapter, visit My eLab.

TAKE ACTION!

WRITING TOPICS

Write about one of the following topics. For more information about how to structure an essay, see Writing Workshop 2 on pages 141-147.

1 Risk-Taking

Write about risk-taking. Structure your essay in the following way:

- Introduce your topic. Do you take risks? Are you an adrenaline junkie? Describe the type of child that you were.

- In your second paragraph, describe someone you know. Choose someone who is not like you. What risks does that person take?

2 Sports in My Country

Write an essay about sports. Your essay should have the following elements:

- Introduce your topic. What are some sports in your country?
- In your first body paragraph, describe why sports are important. You can discuss how sports help individuals. Also consider the value of team sports and national sports. Why do people go to sporting events?
- Use the past tense, and describe a particular sporting game or activity that you saw or that you participated in. When and where did it happen? What exciting moments occurred?
- Write a short conclusion. End with a prediction or suggestion.

SPEAKING TOPICS

Prepare a presentation on one of the following topics.

1 Role Model Interview

Kara Bruce became inspired to try BMX because she learned about a professional BMX rider. Think about someone who inspires you. Choose someone you know.

- Compose ten questions that you would like to ask that person. Use past, present, and future tense verbs in your questions.
- Interview your role model. In a two-minute presentation, give information about that person. Remember to prepare cue cards, and practise before your presentation.

2 Heroes

Discuss people who influenced you in the past and those who influence you today.

- In a short introduction, explain why people have heroes.
- Discuss your heroes when you were a child. Who did you admire? You can talk about real people or about fictional heroes such as Superman.
- Then describe one or more people who influence you today. Who do you admire? Explain why.

SPEAKING PRESENTATION TIPS

- **Practise your presentation and time yourself.** You should speak for about two minutes.
- **Use cue cards.** Do not read! Put about fifteen keywords words on your cue cards.
- **Bring visual support**, such as a picture, photograph, object, video, or PowerPoint slides.
- **Classmates will ask you questions about your presentation.** You must also ask your classmates about their presentations. Review how to form questions before your presentation day.

REVISING AND EDITING

EDIT PLURAL AND ADJECTIVE FORMS AND REVISE FOR A CONCLUSION

Practise editing an essay. Underline and correct nine errors with plural and comparative forms, not including the example. Then write a concluding paragraph. It can be two or three sentences long. (For more information about writing a conclusion, see Writing Workshop 2 on pages 141-147.)

Life is short, and we can have many exciting adventures. Is it a good idea to take risk? (risks) In fact, it is more better to take risks than to be too cautious.

First, when we take risks, we develop perseverance. In the interview with Kara Bruce, we learned that she worried a lots when she was a child. She became bravest than before when she started to ride BMX. She learned to do some trick. After she broke several bones, she did not stop BMX riding. Today, she feels proud that she faced difficults challenges and she persevered.

Second, many parents overprotect their childrens, but persons become more independent when they take risks. In "A Lesson in Brave Parenting," Abby Sunderland was just a sixteen-years-old girl when she started a solo sailing trip. Her parents did not stop her. Abby survived a disaster, and she became more strong.

Conclusion: ______________________________

____

____

____

____

____

GRAMMAR TIP

Plurals

Never add a plural ending to an adjective. Be careful, because some nouns become adjectives when they modify another noun.

noun	adjective
The show costs ten **dollars**.	We have three ten-**dollar** tickets.

To learn more about plural forms, see Unit 5 in *Avenues 1: English Grammar*.

CHAPTER 7

LIFE ONLINE

"Use the Internet to help your daily life, not replace it."

— DAVID CHILES, AUTHOR

How much time do you spend online? How important is social media to you? This chapter examines our online lives.

START UP Tech Life

Social Media

Social media includes Facebook, Instagram, Twitter, Snapchat, and similar sites. Work with a partner or a small group of classmates. Take turns chatting about the following topics. You can change topics at any time. When the teacher flicks the lights on and off, change speakers.

1. The best apps
2. What I don't like about Facebook or another social media site
3. Annoying things people do on social media sites

Life Before the Computer Age

With a partner or team, describe life as it was before the computer age. List two or three ideas for each item. Begin each idea with a past tense verb.

ACTIVITY	BEFORE THE COMPUTER AGE
Shopping online (e.g., eBay)	▪ went to grocery stores ▪ shopped in malls ▪ phoned in orders
Sharing life details (e.g., Facebook)	
Posting photos online (e.g., Instagram, Snapchat)	
Dating online (e.g., Tinder, Plenty of Fish)	
Researching online (e.g., Google)	
Playing online games	

READING 7.1 WITH LISTENING

COULD YOU LIVE WITHOUT YOUR PHONE? In this narrative blog, Merlin Barry describes the ways his phone is changing him.

GRAMMAR LINK

As you read, you will see some word choices in parentheses. Underline the correct word (*X* means "nothing"). In My eLab, you can listen to this essay and check your answers. As you read along, pay attention to the speaker's intonation and pronunciation.

I Am a Phone Addict

BY MERLIN BARRY

1 I am addicted to my phone. I text constantly. I play stupid and brainless games. I check updates (on / at) Instagram or Facebook obsessively. I read headlines on Flipboard. And as a recently separated parent, heaven help me, I now have Tinder. I am not a child or a teen. I am a forty-four-year-old, so I have lived in the pre-texting/Facebook/Instagram world. I am ashamed to admit (than / that) my phone is making me a less patient and focused person.

You can prepare for your reading tests by trying the reading strategies on pages 132-136. You can also practise by visiting My eLab. Click on Reading Strategies to find a variety of exercises.

2 I remember the days before a cellphone was attached to my hand. Twenty years ago, my only phone was connected to my kitchen wall. Out in the world, I spoke to people, looked in their eyes, and listened (at / to / X) them. I recall when phone answering machines were the biggest distraction to communication. We played "phone tag," leaving messages for each other on answering machines, then laughing about it later.

lure: attraction

3 For years, I resisted the **lure** of mobile phones. But in 1998, I finally broke down and bought one of those flip-screen (model / models). For months, I was vaguely uncomfortable with the notion that someone could contact me (at / in / on) any time of day. The first few times the phone rang when I was in the checkout line at the grocery store or in a workplace meeting, I felt embarrassed and even mildly violated. "Not now," I wanted to shout at the unknown caller.

4 The initial discomfort passed (quick / quickly). I upgraded phones every few years, and my phone is now part of my body. I am never without it. I use my phone throughout the day, and it is on my bedside table at night.

skim: read quickly

characters: individual letters and spaces (Twitter posts are a maximum of 140 characters.)

5 Unfortunately, my phone is contributing to my shorter attention span. I used (to / X) read books in bed, and I devoured a couple of novels a month. But something happened to me. Maybe I **skim** too many headlines, Twitter feeds, Facebook posts, and Instagram comments, but my focused attention can't exceed 140 **characters** or so. That's sad.

6 These days, I require non-stop stimulation. In the past, if I had nothing to do, I could stare at the clouds and reflect. Now, I open a game app and slide candy around the screen. If I'm waiting at a traffic light, I pull out the phone, check my messages, and reply to them. I know it's (illegal / illegally) and dangerous to text in the car, but I hate waiting for anything or anyone. Waiting is boring, and I have my phone to relieve my boredom.

7 I make (quicker / quickly) and more impulsive judgments. In the dating world, when I met my first partner, I had to—you know—meet her and speak with her

cursory: rapid

and get to know her. Now, with Tinder, I swipe left or right based on a face pic. After a **cursory** message, we arrange to meet. Then, if I'm disappointed—she's not as cute (than / as) her picture, or she's too talkative, or ... whatever—I move on to the next person.

8 I love my phone, but I also hate it. It fulfills my need for constant stimulation and gratification. At any moment, I can play a game or look for a wife. Who wouldn't love that? Yet, I know that it is reducing my attention span and changing my interactions with fellow human beings. My phone is chipping away at my heart and limiting my world to a small screen. And that, I really don't like.

(566 words)

COMPREHENSION

VOCABULARY

1 Which phone is a flip-screen model? Circle the letter of the best answer.

a. b. c.  d. 

2 Find a verb in paragraph 3 that means "speak loudly." ____________

3 Find a verb in paragraph 7 that means "move a finger across (a touchscreen) to activate a function." ____________

MAIN AND SUPPORTING IDEAS

4 The thesis expresses the main point of this essay. Look in the introduction, and highlight the thesis.

5 When did Barry first buy a cellphone? ____________

6 Initially, how did Barry feel about cellphones? ____________

____

____

7 How is Barry different now that he has a cellphone? List three major changes in his behaviour. ____________

____

____

____

WRITING

Write about your own cellphone usage. When did you get your first cellphone? Are you a phone addict?

SPEAKING One-Day Tech Challenge

What are your tech habits? Could you give up your phone or computer for a day? Work with a partner or team, and try the following activity.

PART 1

First, answer the questions below. Then share your answers with your partner or teammates.

1 What tech devices do you own or have access to? (Put a checkmark beside each device you own or use.)

___ smartphone ___ tablet ___ laptop ___ desktop computer

2 How often do you check your phone each day?

a. never
b. one to five times
c. five to fifteen times
d. so many times I can't count

3 What social media sites do you visit on a regular basis? (Put a checkmark beside all the sites you use.)

___ Facebook ___ Instagram ___ Snapchat
___ Twitter Other: ______________________________

4 What do you do most often online? Number the items from 1 (most often) to 6 (least often).

___ go on social media
___ text people
___ play games
___ read news, etc.
___ watch videos
___ be creative (write, make music, take photos, videos)

5 Make a prediction. Will you be able to spend a whole day without using your tech devices? Why or why not?

____

____

____

PART 2

Choose either a Saturday or a Sunday, and try to live without your phone, tablet, or computer. When you wake up, put your gadgets away, and see how many hours you can last. (If you must use your phone, try to use it only to speak: no texting or using an app. Use your computer only to do homework.)

WRITING

Write an essay about your tech habits. First, describe how you use your technological devices. Then explain how you reacted to the "no tech" challenge. Could you do it? If not, explain why not.

WATCHING 7.1 Distracted Drivers

Distracted driving kills. How serious is texting and driving? Watch and find out.

COMPREHENSION

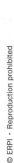

1 CBC News host Reg Sherren said, "A recent American study found four states where texting while driving is now illegal." What happened in those states after it became illegal?

a. Accident rates went down.

b. Accident rates stayed the same.

c. Accident rates increased.

2 At the time of the video, Winnipeg created a new law prohibiting texting and driving. What is the result, according to Sergeant Rob Riffel?

a. People started driving more safely.

b. People were even more distracted because they were trying to hide their actions.

3 Texting while driving can be up to . . . times more dangerous than drunk driving.

a. two b. three c. five d. ten

4 In Manitoba, the law on texting while driving is . . . than the law on drinking and driving.

a. more severe b. less severe

5 At the time this video was made, what was the penalty for texting while driving in Manitoba?

a. a ticket b. driver's licence revoked c. prison

6 According to Liz Peters from CAA Manitoba, sixteen- to nineteen-year-olds have . . . more accidents than people aged forty-five or over.

a. ten times b. twenty times c. a hundred times

7 A woman was caught texting while driving her red SUV. Who was she texting? ____________

8 In Utah, Reggie Shaw had an accident. What happened? ____________

____

____

9 What law did New Jersey introduce to deal with distracted driving?

____

____

10 What was Dillon Poberezhsky doing when a truck hit him?

a. skateboarding b. riding his bike c. walking

DISCUSSION

1 Why do people text when they are driving?

2 Should penalties for texting while driving be as severe as those for drinking and driving? Why or why not?

3 Why could New Jersey's new law be difficult to enforce?

VOCABULARY **BOOST**

Social Media Terms

Practise using social media vocabulary. (Note that many of these words have different meanings in another context.) Write the letters of the best definitions in the spaces provided.

My eLab

The Chapter Review exercise in My eLab offers more practice with technology-related vocabulary.

Terms		Definitions
1. block	_____	a. self-portrait that is posted online
2. hashtag	_____	b. number of visitors that a site receives
3. GIF	_____	c. prevent from viewing your Facebook profile
4. selfie	_____	d. remove as a friend on Facebook
5. traffic	_____	e. something shared online rapidly
6. tweet	_____	f. small (compressed) digital image file
7. unfriend	_____	g. word or phrase preceded by #
8. viral	_____	h. short (140-character) message on Twitter

READING 7.2

HOW IMPORTANT IS SOCIAL MEDIA TO YOU? Peggy Drexler is a research psychologist at Cornell University. In the following essay, she discusses the impact of social media.

My eLab

You can prepare for your reading tests by trying the reading strategies on pages 132-136. You can also practise by visiting My eLab. Click on Reading Strategies to find a variety of exercises.

Your Social Life Is Not Your Social Media

BY PEGGY DREXLER, PhD

1 Jessie, a thirty-year-old real estate agent, was the last of her friends to join Instagram. The day she signed up, she followed sixty accounts—friends and acquaintances as well as accounts maintained by clothing brands or celebrities she was interested in. Then she busily posted photos. By the end of the month, she was following more than two hundred accounts, most of them people she actually knew. But she amassed only fifteen followers of her own. She wondered why some friends didn't follow her. "I took it very personally," she told me. "Was it that they thought my life was so boring that it wasn't worth following? Or were we not really friends after all?"

2 Well, it could be both, or it could be neither. Perhaps her friends were trying to send her a message. Maybe they didn't really like her. Perhaps they thought her life was **dull** beyond belief. Or maybe it is something far more benign. Maybe her friends don't take social media as seriously as she does and would be surprised

dull: boring

to learn they had hurt her. The intention no longer mattered: Jessie began to question relationships she had felt fine with just weeks earlier.

angst: anxiety

3 Social media-induced **angst** is happening with increasing frequency. Just as businesses and brands use social media to monitor consumer interest, people use social media to gauge how their friends and acquaintances feel about them. "Likes" may be interpreted as approvals. Not "liking," not following, or otherwise not engaging might translate into snubs. Social media etiquette is largely undefined, and there are few universally understood and followed rules. Interpretation is highly subjective and, in many instances, leans toward the worst-case scenario.

fuel: feed; stimulate

4 Social media makes many aspects of relationships more accessible. Viewing posts from friends scattered around the world can make us feel more connected to them. Online, it can be easier to get in touch with someone than with more traditional, offline means. But social media also helps **fuel** feelings of isolation and self-doubt. A 2012 study published in the journal *Cyberpsychology, Behavior, and Social Networking*, for example, found that the longer people spent on Facebook each week, the more they agreed that everyone else was happier and had better lives.

countered: opposed; resisted

5 For some, that self-doubt can be **countered** in the same place it originates: through affirming social media interactions. Part of what keeps users coming back to sites like Instagram and Facebook is the favourable attention. When likes accumulate, it is an addictive sort of reward. It's also what makes not receiving those affirmations so dispiriting. Negative feelings are exacerbated when friends don't follow us back. It can feel devastating if a friend stops following us, unfriends us, or—worst of all—blocks us.

6 If social media endorsements do not arrive, people can develop feelings of anxiety, inadequacy, and irritation. For instance, Ben fulfilled a lifelong dream of opening a bookstore and created a business page on Facebook. Then he invited all 750 of his friends to "like" it. Barely a quarter of them did. Every day, as he monitored his page waiting for the likes that didn't come, he grew more and more offended. He always remembered his friend Lisa's daughter's birthday! He was a caring friend to Danny. And what happened with Mike, his best man? Friendship, for Ben, became scorekeeping. When those friends who let him down on social media called on him in real life, Ben became cool and distant.

7 It's normal to feel irritated when a friend responds to another friend's tweets, but never yours. And it's understandable to feel jealous when you see photos of two friends having fun together at a concert when you sat home watching Netflix, unaware that they had made plans without you. It's even a new sort of normal to upload a retaliatory "good time pic" of your own.

shallow: superficial; not profound

8 But social media is a **shallow** barometer of friendship. It's unrealistic and dangerous to presume we know how someone feels about us based on how they react through virtual means. How people use social media is too new and too varied. Judging how someone feels about us is what face-to-face encounters are for. It's called real life.

(583 words)

Source:

Drexler, Peggy. "Your Social Life Is Not Your Social Media." *Our Gender, Ourselves*. Psychology Today, 17 Oct. 2013. Web.

COMPREHENSION

GRAMMAR LINK Unscramble the words in each question. Then answer the question.

Example: Jessie / when / join Instagram / did? When did Jessie join Instagram?
Answer: She joined Instagram when she was thirty.

1. why / Jessie / feel bad / did? ______

   Answer (paragraph 1): ______

2. what / snubs / does / mean? ______

   Answer (paragraph 3):

   a. rich people b. happy feelings c. affronts or insults

3. one benefit / what / is / of social media? ______

   Answer (paragraph 4): ______

4. what / endorsements / are? ______

   Answer (paragraph 6):

   a. affirmations; support b. publicity c. friends

5. Ben / what job / does / do? ______

   Answer (paragraph 6): ______

6. why / Ben / become angry / did? ______

   Answer (paragraph 6): ______

7. the writer's / what / main point / is? ______

   Answer: ______

WATCHING 7.2 The Power of Online Shaming

These days, if we make a mistake in a public place, there is always a risk that someone will film us. What follows could be public shaming. Watch as CBC discusses this all-too-common problem and its consequences.

PRE-WATCHING VOCABULARY

Review these terms and definitions before you watch the video.

- **fine:** money that someone must pay as a penalty for a criminal offence
- **club (e.g., an animal):** hit with a piece of wood or another solid object
- **public shaming:** punishing someone in a public or online space

COMPREHENSION

VOCABULARY

1 Watch the video. Then write the missing words in the blanks. Choose from the following list.

bus campaigns fish forget how far

In an era of lightning-fast mass communications, everything can become instantly public, from your proudest moments to the ones you'd rather __________. And the world is there eager to act as judge and jury. Public shaming __________ have become more and more commonplace, from the guy who won't give up his seat on the __________ to the man who killed a __________. Havard Gould looks at __________ public shaming can go.

MAIN AND SUPPORTING IDEAS

2 What illegal act did Eddie Parent commit? __________

3 What did another fisherman do to Eddie? __________

4 The host says that "Eddie escalated everything by mouthing off." What does *mouthing off* mean?

a. covering his mouth b. crying c. boasting loudly

5 After the video went viral, what did Eddie do? __________

6 Eddie received two formal punishments. What were they? __________

7. According to this report, more than . . . people viewed the video of Eddie and the fish.

a. 50,000 b. 100,000 c. 300,000 d. a million

8 Eddy is "mocked and recognized endlessly." What does *mocked* mean?

a. ridiculed b. loved c missed d. false

9 The video mentions three other people who were publically shamed in the US. What did they do?

____

My eLab

Answer additional questions for all the reading and listening activities on My eLab. You can also access audio and video clips online.

10 Jennifer Jacquet gives an example of positive public shaming. What is the example? ____

____

DISCUSSION

1 What is your opinion about the shaming of Eddie Parent and others?

2 Should governments use public shaming to make people do positive actions?

SPEAKING Social Media Etiquette

Work with a partner or team, and discuss social media etiquette. Consider the types of posts that you find annoying. Also think about problems such as blocking, unfriending, and cyberbullying. Then create rules for social media usage. List the rules on a separate piece of paper. You can include reasons for the rules, or present possible consequences if people don't follow the rules.

Example: Don't post political videos because you will lose friends.

GRAMMAR TIP

Giving Commands

You can use the imperative form to give a command. Use just the base form of the verb. To form the negative, put *do not* or *don't* before the verb. (*You should/should not* is implied but not stated.)

Post funny videos.

Don't write really long text messages.

To learn more about imperatives and the simple present, see Unit 2 in *Avenues 1: English Grammar.*

READING 7.3

"THE MAGIC APP" IS A SHORT STORY ABOUT TIME. Read the story, and imagine what you would do in the main character's place.

TEAM READING ACTIVITY (OPTIONAL)

Work with five other people, and form pairs. There are three parts to "The Magic App." Each pair of students could read Part 1, Part 2, or Part 3. Answer the questions after your part. Later, you can share information with your team.

My eLab

You can prepare for your reading tests by trying the reading strategies on pages 132-136. You can also practise by visiting My eLab. Click on Reading Strategies to find a variety of exercises.

The Magic App

PART 1

1 Once there was a ten-year-old boy, Luke, who had dark hair and bright eyes. He hated school, and he always daydreamed during class. "Luke, what are you dreaming about this time?" his teacher would ask.

2 "I'm thinking about what I'll be when I grow up," Luke replied.

3 "Be patient. Being grown up isn't always fun, you know," his teacher said.

4 But Luke was impatient to finish school. During the week, he thought about the weekend. In the winter, he looked forward to the warm days of summer.

5 One chilly winter evening, while he was reclining on his bed, he picked up his phone. He was about to text a friend when the screen turned white.

6 From his phone, a robotic voice spoke. "Luke, this magic app is for you. Nobody else in the world has it." On his screen appeared the words *Flash Forward* above a shining gold ball. "Is this a virus?" Luke wondered. The voice continued, "You can remove this app, and time will pass normally. But if you want time to pass quickly, tap the golden ball. Tap it once, and an hour will feel like a second. Tap a couple of times, and a whole day will pass. You will remember what happened during the missing time, but you can never go back and relive that time. Do you accept?"

hoax: trick; deception

7 Luke still thought it might be a **hoax**. He hesitated and said, "Yes."

8 The robotic voice sounded satisfied: "This must be our secret. If you tell anyone else, you will die instantly."

9 Luke—feeling curious—stared at the gold ball. He tapped it, and the sky instantly darkened. "Wow," he thought. "This is real!"

droned: talked in a boring, monotonous tone

10 The following day at school, the teacher's voice **droned** on, and Luke longed for the school day to end. He carefully held his phone under his desk and opened the flash-forward app. He tapped the ball. Suddenly, the teacher was saying, "Pack up your books and leave the classroom in an orderly fashion." Luke was thrilled! He would never again have to listen to a boring teacher!

11 A few months later, when frost appeared on the windows, it occurred to Luke that he could tap until the school year was over. He opened the app and tapped away. He looked outdoors and saw budding flowers and leafy trees. It was June!

stubble: short growth of a beard

12 That summer, Luke resisted the urge to use the app. But when September arrived, school began again. He hated his new teacher and some mean classmates. He detested everything about school, and he wanted to be an adult. "Everyone would skip high school if they could," he decided. That evening, he opened the flash-forward app and tapped furiously. Then he looked down and saw hairy legs and large feet. He stared in the mirror and was astonished to see **stubble** on his chin. How old was he now?

(477 words)

COMPREHENSION

1 Describe the magic app. ______________________

____

2 Why did Luke want to skip past his school years? ______________________

____

3 What will happen if Luke tells someone about the magic app? ______________________

____

PART 2

13 The date on Luke's phone was seven years later. He felt a little dizzy and confused. He realized that he could remember his high school years even though he had not experienced them. His high school graduation certificate was on the wall. The posters and toys of his childhood had been replaced with sports equipment and a new computer. In his hand was a shiny new phone, and the magic app was on it! At the top left of the screen was the gold ball, the symbol for the flash-forward app.

14 That summer of his eighteenth year, he fell madly in love with his friend Ava. She had long red hair and freckles, she wore colourful dresses, and she had an infectious laugh. She was a delightful companion. They discussed their plans to live together and get married in four years, but first, Ava wanted to study abroad. She had a scholarship to study in Switzerland. Luke could not afford to follow her. He needed to stay and attend university closer to home. They promised to remain faithful to each other and to stay in touch online.

15 Luke studied accounting. At first, he enjoyed his classes, and he especially liked the weekend parties. He bought an old car, but he had to work part-time to pay for university tuition and his car loan. In the summer, he worked full time at a service station. By the second year, the repetitive routine became depressing: school, study, work. Even partying became boring without Ava.

16 By December, he was exhausted from his job and studies, and he missed Ava terribly. One evening, he opened the magic app. He tapped and tapped, knowing the days would fly by. Suddenly, Ava appeared before him. She was smiling and talking about their upcoming wedding. Luke's university years were over, and Ava was back!

17 The next summer, Ava and Luke had a fabulous wedding. At the reception dinner, Luke noticed that his dad's hair was gray. With a shock, Luke realized that his father was becoming an old man. Time was moving too quickly! He vowed to use the app only when it was strictly necessary.

18 Luke found a job with the city administration, and Ava developed a career as a successful interior designer. When Ava became pregnant, Luke was overjoyed. Their child, Hans, was delightful, and Luke was mostly content. However, sometimes when the child cried through the night, Luke would tap the ball. When Ava had to travel for business and Luke was alone with their **cranky** son, he tapped a little more. Luke longed to confide in Ava about the app, but he remembered the warning. He didn't want to die, so he kept the app a secret.

(469 words)

cranky: grumpy; bad-tempered

COMPREHENSION

4 Can Luke remember what happened during the period when time flashed forward? Explain your answer. ______________________________

____

5 On what occasions did Luke use the magic app? ______________________________

____

____

6 How does Luke feel at the end of this section? ______________________________

____

PART 3

borrow: take something with the intention of returning it

19 When Luke was thirty-five, an economic crisis occurred. Ava lost her job, and the bank threatened to repossess their home. Desperate, Luke decided to "**borrow**" money from work. As the accountant, he was able to create fake employee profiles and transfer their "earnings" to his bank account. He covered up the fraud by altering the accounting software. Then he paid off his mortgage. Because the money was so easy to obtain, he also took some vacations to beach resorts. For about five years, Luke forgot about the app and enjoyed life.

20 One day, the city had an audit, and Luke's crimes were discovered. He had stolen over a million dollars! Ava was furious with Luke. After a short trial, Luke was sentenced to ten years in prison. Luckily, he had his magic app. Before the prison officials could confiscate his phone, he tapped furiously on the golden ball. The prison walls dissolved around him.

21 Luke, now fifty, found himself alone. Ava was with another man, and Hans was a college student. With his criminal record, Luke couldn't find a job, and he became depressed. His father had died while Luke was in prison, and his mother was now elderly.

ailing: unhealthy; sick

22 Luke moved in with his **ailing** mother and took care of her. He ignored his app because tapping it would only hasten his mother's death. When his mother died, Luke stood at her graveside and realized that his life was slipping away. That night, he determined to remove the app. In tears, he hit the delete "x" repeatedly. Suddenly, the phone screen became white. The robotic voice spoke: "Luke, have you had a good life?"

23 "I'm not sure. At first, the app seemed wonderful. I never had to suffer or wait for anything. But my life passed too quickly." Luke replied. "If I tap the ball again, it will only bring me closer to my death. I hate this magic app!"

24 "You are very ungrateful," the voice said. "But I can give you one last wish, you **foolish** man! "

25 "What can I wish for?" Luke asked.

26 "You choose," the voice said.

27 Luke thought hard. Then he said, "I would like to live my life again as if for the first time, but without the magic app. I'll experience the good times, bad times, and boring times. I want to experience everything."

28 "So be it," said the voice.

29 Luke looked at his phone, and the icon for "Forward Time" was gone. Exhausted, he closed his eyes.

30 When he awoke, his youthful mother was leaning over him. "You were having a nightmare," his mother said. "Everything will be okay."

31 That morning, on his way to school, he noticed the sun glinting on the yellow leaves. He heard the laughter of children running to catch the school bus. Soon he would see his teacher and classmates. The prospect of boring lessons didn't seem so bad. In fact, he could hardly wait.

(484 words)

COMPREHENSION

7 In paragraph 19, why is *borrow* in quotation marks? ____________________

____

8 How did the economic crisis affect Luke? Explain your answer. ____________

____

____

9 Why did Ava leave Luke? Make a guess. ____________________

____

____

10 What is the lesson, or message, of this story? ____________________

____

____

READING GROUP ACTIVITY

Work with a team of about five other students. Choose a partner from your team. Each pair of students should choose one of the following activities. Work with your partner to complete the activity. Then rejoin your team and share your work.

Group 1: Questions

With your partner, compose eight questions about the story. Do not copy any of the questions that appear after each part. Then divide a piece of paper into eight pieces. Write your questions on one side of the paper and the answers on the other side. Use a variety of question words.

When you rejoin your teammates, show them the questions one at a time. Your teammates must try to answer each question. Then you can turn each paper over and show the answers.

Group 2: Definitions

With your partner, choose eight difficult words from the story. Then, on small pieces of paper, write the difficult words on one side and the definitions on the other side.

When you rejoin your other teammates, show them the words in sequence. Your teammates must guess what each word means. Then you can turn each paper over to show the answer.

Group 3: Story Arc

With your partner, write ten sentences that sum up the story. Do not take sentences directly from the text; instead, create your own sentences. Put your sentences in chronological order. Cut a paper into ten parts, and write one sentence on each piece of paper.

When you join the rest of the group, the other team members must put the parts of the story in the correct order.

DISCUSSION AND WRITING

Discuss the following topics. Then choose two topics, and write a paragraph about each one. Give each paragraph a title.

- Why did the boy agree to use the magic app?
- What messages does the story convey? Explain your answer.
- Would you want a magic app to move time forward? Why or why not?

GRAMMAR TIP

Using *Would*

Use *would* to indicate a possibility or desire. Use the base form of the verb after *would*.

I **would love** the app. My brother **would use** it too.

To learn more about modal auxiliaries, see Unit 8 in *Avenues 1: English Grammar*.

LISTENING PRACTICE

1. Pronounce Words

Practise pronouncing the words at the top of page 128. Pay attention to the pronunciation of the letters *h* and *th*. Read the following Pronunciation Tip.

PRONUNCIATION TIP

Pronouncing *t* and *th*

When you pronounce *t*, the tip of your tongue touches the roof of your mouth. But when you pronounce *th*, the tip of your tongue should touch your top teeth.

Example bat bath

Repeat each pair of words after the speaker. Then you will hear a sentence. Underline the word that you hear in the sentence.

1 tank	thank	5 three	tree	9 taught	thought
2 ear	hear	6 air	hair	10 bat	bath
3 math	mat	7 harm	arm		
4 hate	ate	8 tear	there		

2. Spelling

Practise your spelling. Listen to the speaker and fill in the missing words.

1 Some ________ love to have risky ________________.

2 For ____________, Kara rides her BMX in ____________.

3 She ____________ puts ____________ on Instagram.

4 I will probably ride ________ her ____________.

5 The ____________ old trees are ____________.

6 She lives in an ________________ with her ____________.

7 I ____________ that her mother ____________ math.

8 My brother ____________ a ball ____________ the window.

9 The Smiths sold ________ car to my ____________.

10 Yes, ____________ are great ____________ in this college.

LISTENING Finding Love Online

Navid Khavari ventured into the world of online dating. In this interview with Sook-Yin Lee, he discusses a date with a woman he met online. Listen to the interview, and do the following exercise.

COMPREHENSION

Write a paragraph about Navid Khavari's dating experience. In your paragraph, include the following information.

- Which dating site did he use, and why?
- What happened on the first date? Provide details.
- Why did the woman feel comfortable with Navid?

SPEAKING Dating World

Work with a team, and discuss the following questions. Then write a paragraph about your conclusions.

1 In the past, did you go on Tinder or another dating site?

2 What is your opinion of dating sites and apps?

3 Is there a stigma if you meet someone online? Why or why not?

4 What mistakes do people make on their online dating profiles?

WRITING

Write ten questions that you would ask a potential romantic partner. Use the past, present, and future tenses in your questions. Also use at least one modal auxiliary (*can*, *would*, *should*, etc.). Out of respect for your teacher, do not ask inappropriate questions.

GRAMMAR TIP

Questions with *How*

Use *how* to create a variety of questions.

Question words	Refer to	
How old	age	**How old** are you?
How far	distance	**How far** is your city from here?
How long	length of time	**How long** did you spend in high school?
How often	frequency	**How often** do you travel?
How much/many	quantity	**How much** does the wine cost?
		How many children do you have?

For more information about question forms, see Unit 4 in *Avenues 1: English Grammar*.

TAKE ACTION!

WRITING TOPICS

Write about one of the following topics. For information about paragraph structure, see Writing Workshop I on pages 137-140.

1 Phone Apps

Write about phone apps. First, describe an app that you used in the past. Why was it so good? How did you use it? Then, in a second paragraph, describe your current favourite app. (Use your own words, and do not borrow words or phrases from websites.)

2 Technology in My Life

Write an essay about your experience with technology and social media. Include the following elements.

- In two or three sentences, introduce your topic.

- Explain the role of technology and media in your past. How old were you when you first used a computer? When did you first receive a cellphone? During your childhood, did you spend a lot of time playing online or video games? How did technological devices impact your childhood?
- Describe your current use of tech devices. What do you do online each day? Are you addicted to social media? Why or why not?
- Conclude with a suggestion or prediction.

SPEAKING TOPICS

Prepare a presentation about one of the following topics.

1 Technology

Discuss one of the following topics.

a. Present the evolution of a type of technology. Show examples of older versions of that technology, and demonstrate how it changed over the years.

b. Argue that a certain device (phone, laptop, etc.) makes our lives better or worse.

c. Argue that certain apps or social media sites make our lives better or worse.

2 A Problem in Society

Present a problem in society. Choose something that you know well.

Possible topics include: body image, drug use, dropout rates, drinking and driving, addictions, environmental problems, or your choice.

- Begin with a personal story about the problem. Describe what happened to you, someone you know, or someone who is well known. Give details.
- Then suggest a solution. What should people do about the problem?
- In your conclusion, explain what you will teach your children.

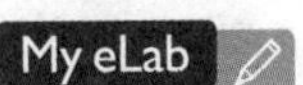

To practise vocabulary from this chapter, visit My eLab.

3 Public Service Announcement Video

Work alone or with a partner. Videotape a public service announcement. Your announcement should be about two minutes long. Convince viewers to be careful. Choose one of the following topics:

- Texting while driving
- Cyberbullying
- An addiction (drugs, social networking, etc.)
- Your own topic

SPEAKING PRESENTATION TIPS

- **Practise your presentation and time yourself.** You should speak for about two minutes.
- **Use cue cards.** Do not read! Put about fifteen keywords on your cue cards.
- **Bring visual support**, such as a picture, photograph, object, video, or PowerPoint slides.
- **Classmates will ask you questions about your presentation.** You must also ask your classmates about their presentations. Review how to form questions before your presentation day.

REVISING AND EDITING

REVISE FOR SENTENCE VARIETY

A piece of writing should contain some sentence variety. In the next essay, use the following words to combine some sentences.

and   so   but   even though   when

Example: He took risks~~. He~~ , and tried car-surfing.

I made a big mistake. I was fifteen. I took the car. I didn't have my licence. I just wanted to drive. My parents were not home. The keys were on the table. I asked my twin brother to come with me. I was scared. We got in the car and drove around the neighbourhood. Suddenly, while I was driving, my phone rang. I decided to answer the phone.

EDIT FOR MIXED ERRORS

Underline and correct ten errors. Look for errors in comparisons, plurals, verb tense, and subject-verb agreement. Also look for one capitalization error. (See the Grammar Tip box for information about comparisons.)

While I was texting, my foot pressed on the gas. The car went more faster than before. I didn't knew how to brake correctly. I lost control and two others cars almost hit us. Later, when we arrived home, ours parents was in the house. They looked furious.

My father grounded me for three weeks. I cannot go out on weekends. After that, I did not drove for two years. I waited until i had a driver's licence. I wanted to be a more better driver before I was using the car again.

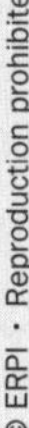

GRAMMAR TIP

Adjectives

In comparisons, do not add *more* and *-er* to an adjective. Just add *-er* to short adjectives. Also remember that adjectives never take a plural form.

Ben is ~~more~~ younger than the ~~others~~ other students.

To learn more about the comparative forms of adjectives, see Unit 10 in *Avenues 1: English Grammar.*

Visit My eLab for more practice trying the different reading strategies.

Vocabulary

When you read, you expand your vocabulary and you learn how English writers develop ideas. Review the following tips. Note that you can practise these strategies online in My eLab.

Visit My eLab for more practice using context clues.

Recognizing Context Clues

When you read a document and come across a new word, what do you do? If you constantly have to use a dictionary or glossary, it can slow down your reading and make you feel frustrated. But if you skip over difficult words, you might not understand what you read.

An effective way to determine a word's meaning is to use context clues. Context clues are hints that help clarify a word's meanings. Look for context clues in a text by following these steps:

1. Look at the parts of the word. You might recognize a part of the word and be able to guess the meaning (*hairdresser*).
2. Determine the part of speech. Sometimes it helps to know a word's function. Is it a noun, a verb, an adjective, and so on? For example, *His night shift ended at 8 a.m.* You know that *shift* is a noun. This can help you guess its meaning.
3. Look at surrounding words and sentences. Look for a synonym (a word that has the same meaning) or an antonym (a word that has the opposite meaning). Also look at surrounding sentences, and use logic to deduce, or guess, the word's meaning.

PRACTICE 1

1. Determine the meaning of the words in bold.

   a. Some consumers buy **trendy** clothes. Two months later, the trend is over and the fashion item is relegated to the bottom of the closet.

   Part of speech: a. adjective b. noun c. verb

   Clue: ______________________________

   Meaning: ______________________________

   b. Mr. and Mrs. Perez are extremely excited because their business **is booming**! They have more customers every day.

   Part of speech: a. adjective b. noun c. verb

   Clue: ______________________________

   Meaning: ______________________________

2 Read the paragraph. Use context clues to help you determine the definition of the words in bold. Circle the letter of the best definition.

Price bundling means selling two or more goods or services as a single package for one price. Companies lure consumers into buying more than they planned. A music buff can buy tickets to an entire concert series for a single price. A PC typically comes bundled with a monitor, a keyboard, and software.

Source: Solomon, M. R., *Marketing: Real People, Real Choices*. Upper Saddle River: Pearson, 2008. 356. Print.

1. bundling:	a. opening	b. holding	c. grouping together
2. lure:	a. tempt	b. write	c. send
3. buff:	a. hater	b. enthusiast	c. instrument
4. tickets:	a. music	b. money	c. admission coupons
5. entire:	a. great	b. complete	c. cost

Recognizing Slang and Idiomatic Expressions

Slang is informal "street" language.

Slang: My **bro** and I are going to eat some **grub** and **chill**.
Standard English: My **brother** and I are going to eat some **food** and **relax**.

Idiomatic expressions have meanings that do not match the meaning of the individual words.

Idiomatic expression: That job is a **piece of cake**.
Meaning: That job is **easy**.

PRACTICE 2

Use context clues to guess the meanings of the slang and idiomatic expressions in bold.

Example: That new iPhone costs **an arm and a leg**. I can't afford it.

a lot of money

1 My sister **freaked out** when her boyfriend broke up with her. We could not calm her down. ______________

2 My friends **hang out** at the coffee shop. They spend hours drinking one cup of coffee. ______________

3 Craig and Julia's new dog **trashed** their apartment. It destroyed the furniture. ______________

4 We are going to **hit the road** next year. We plan to go to Guatemala and Honduras. ______________

Identifying Cognates (Word Twins)

Many languages share words that have the same linguistic root. Cognates—or word twins—are words that have a similar appearance and meaning in different languages.

Example: English: visit French: visite Spanish and Italian: visita

False Cognates

Be careful, because some English words look similar to words in your language, but they have different meanings. For example, in English, *attend* means "go to" (I attended the conference). The French word *attendre* means "wait."

PRACTICE 3

Read the following paragraphs and underline words that look like words in your language.

When a crisis happens and a person is in pain, what is a sensible way to react? Is it useful to cry and scream? Or is it better to be stoic and show self-control?

Many medical professionals now agree that there is a mind-body link. Depression and sadness can actually affect the immune system.

Fill in the chart below with five of the words that you underlined. Include at least two false cognates (words that look like words in your language but have different meanings).

	Spelling in English	Spelling in my language	The meaning	
			Same	Different
1	______________	______________	☐	☐
2	______________	______________	☐	☐
3	______________	______________	☐	☐
4	______________	______________	☐	☐
5	______________	______________	☐	☐

Using a Dictionary

Use a dictionary only when you cannot understand a word from the context in which it appears. When you consult a dictionary, remember to follow these steps:

- **Determine the part of speech.** For instance, imagine that you do not know the meaning of *fine* in the sentence, "He received a fine." Your dictionary gives three definitions: fine (adj.), fine (n.), and fine (v.). Look at the noun definition.
- **Read all of the meanings and choose the logical one.** Some words have more than one definition. For example, wind means "blowing air," but it also means "bend or turn." Read the word in context and you should be able to identify the correct definition.

Online and Electronic Resources

Online, you will find many dictionary and thesaurus sites. For instance, *dictionary.reference.com* provides definitions, and you can click on the loudspeaker icon to hear how a word is pronounced. Furthermore, many smartphone apps offer word meanings, synonyms, antonyms, and even translations. Also, check your word processing program. It has a built-in dictionary and thesaurus functionality that can help you as you write. For example, in Word, you can right-click on words, and a menu appears that includes a definition, synonym, and translation. (Ensure that you change your version of Word to English by clicking on "Tools" and "Language.")

PRACTICE 4

Use your dictionary—or go to *dictionary.reference.com*—to define the words in bold. Check multiple definitions, and consider the part of speech before you write your definition.

1. The giraffes live in the *wild*. ______________________________
2. Do not go near the *wild* dog. ______________________________
3. The hunters decided to *pelt* the protestors with rocks. ______________________________
4. The actress will not wear an animal *pelt*. ______________________________

General Understanding

Identifying Main and Supporting Ideas

When you read, identify **the main idea**, or principal idea. (If someone asks you what a text is about, your one-sentence summary is a statement of main idea.) Sometimes, the title, introduction, or conclusion expresses the main idea. Often, the main idea appears at the end of the introductory paragraph.

Professional writers do not always express the main point directly. If you cannot find a statement with the main idea, ask yourself *who, what, when, where, why,* and *how* questions. Then, in one or two sentences, write your own statement of main idea.

The supporting ideas are the facts, examples, and details that develop the main idea.

PRACTICE 5

Read the following excerpt, then answer the questions.

> What is an adult? In some cultures, adulthood is the period when a person reaches sexual maturity. But exactly when adulthood begins is not always easy to determine. For some, adulthood can be considered the period of life from the early twenties until old age and death. But in other cultures, adulthood is reached soon after puberty. Some people feel that it begins after graduation from high school, whereas others would say adulthood doesn't begin until after graduation from college. Perhaps adulthood is the point when a person becomes totally self-sufficient with a job and a home separate from his or her parents. In that case, some people are not adults until their late thirties.

Source: Cicarelli, Saundra K. *Psychology*. Upper Saddle River: Pearson, 2009. 342. Print.

My eLab

Visit My eLab for more practice understanding main and supporting ideas.

1 Underline one sentence in the paragraph that shows the main idea.

2 List some supporting ideas.

____

____

____

Identifying the Message

When you look for the main idea, you ask **what** the text is about. When you look for the message, you ask **why** the author wrote the essay. Often, writers express a lesson that they learned. When you read, consider the message.

Sometimes the meaning of a reading is not immediately clear. You must search for the author's message by reading between the lines. In other words, look for clues in the text, and use your logic to make a guess about the author's meaning.

PRACTICE 6

Read the following excerpt, then answer the questions.

> Those close to me recognize that I am a liar. My parents bow their heads sadly when they catch me in another lie. A few months ago, I fibbed when I totalled my dad's car. I said that a child jumped in front of me, and I turned the wheel to avoid her. Really, I was texting while driving. I could tell that my father didn't believe me. My girlfriend also knows that I lie. I sometimes pretend I'm with my friends when I am really talking with another girl. And my best buddy knows I am not honest. One time, I told him I couldn't go out on a Saturday night because I felt sick, but later that evening, he saw me in a club. Now he doesn't trust me. The problem with all of this lying is the guilt. I feel terrible, but I can't stop.

My eLab

Visit My eLab for more practice identifying the message in a text.

1 Underline one sentence in the paragraph that shows the main idea.

2 List some supporting ideas.

____

____

____

3 What is the message of the text? Write down one or two ideas.

____

____

____

Generating Ideas

When you are given a writing assignment, two useful strategies to help you develop your ideas include **brainstorming** and **clustering**.

BRAINSTORMING

Create a list of ideas. Don't worry about grammar or spelling—the point is to generate ideas.

Example: Inexpensive ways to enjoy life

- walk in a park
- drive with the windows open
- sleep in the hot sun
- eat wild raspberries
- make someone laugh really hard

CLUSTERING

Draw an idea in a circle. Then use connecting lines and circles to show your other ideas.

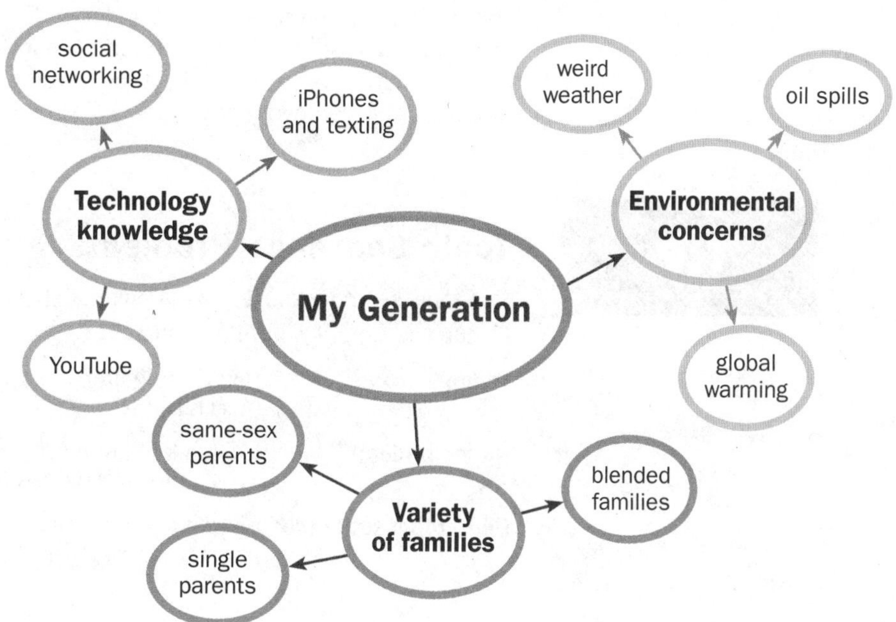

COMPOSE IT

Generate Ideas

Use brainstorming or clustering strategies. Develop ideas related to one of the following topics, or choose your own topic. (Use a separate sheet of paper.)

Bad habits Health Consumer culture

Other topics: ______________________________

The Topic Sentence

A **paragraph** contains one main idea, presented in the **topic sentence**. The other sentences in the paragraph support the main idea. Your topic sentence should have the following qualities.

- It is a complete sentence.
- It is the most general sentence in the paragraph.
- It expresses the topic.
- It contains a main idea that presents the focus of the paragraph.

My lab partner has many interesting qualities.

WRITING EXERCISE 1

Read the following paragraphs. Write a topic sentence for each paragraph.

1 Topic sentence: ______________________________

____

First, take shorter showers. Five minutes is enough time to get clean. Also, only do the laundry when there is a full load. When brushing your teeth, don't leave the water running. Just turn the water on and off as needed. Finally, ask your landlord to install toilets that use very little water.

2 Topic sentence: ______________________________

____

First, children in daycare become independent. They learn to separate from their parents. Also, they are exposed to many viruses, so they develop strong immune systems. Finally, they develop social skills because they play with other children every day.

TIP

Topic Sentence Problems

Your topic sentence must make a point. It should not be vague. Do not write My topic is . . . or I will write about . . . .

Vague:	This is a big problem. (What is a problem? The topic is unclear.)
No main idea:	I will talk about bicycle riders. (What is the main point? This says nothing relevant about the topic.)
Good topic sentence:	Bicycle riders break many traffic laws. (The topic is clear and there is a main idea.)

WRITING EXERCISE 2

Write "OK" under good topic sentences. If the sentence is vague, incomplete, or lacks a focus, rewrite it.

1 I will write about my lab partner.

____

2 Credit cards are dangerous for some people.

____

3 I will write about stress.

____

4 Singing is good for the health.

____

5 This is my dream vacation.

____

COMPOSE IT

Write Topic Sentences

Write a topic sentence for two of the following topics. You can also choose your own topics. Remember to first narrow your topic down to give it a more specific focus.

Bad habits   Health   Consumer culture

Other topics: ______________________________

Example: Topic: Work   Specific topic: Tipping of service workers

Topic sentence: The rules about tipping service workers are not clear.

1. Topic: __________ Specific topic: __________

   Topic sentence: ______________________________

2. Topic: __________ Specific topic: __________

   Topic sentence: ______________________________

The Supporting Ideas

When you finish writing the topic sentence, you must think of specific evidence that supports it. You can include facts, anecdotes, examples, and reasons.

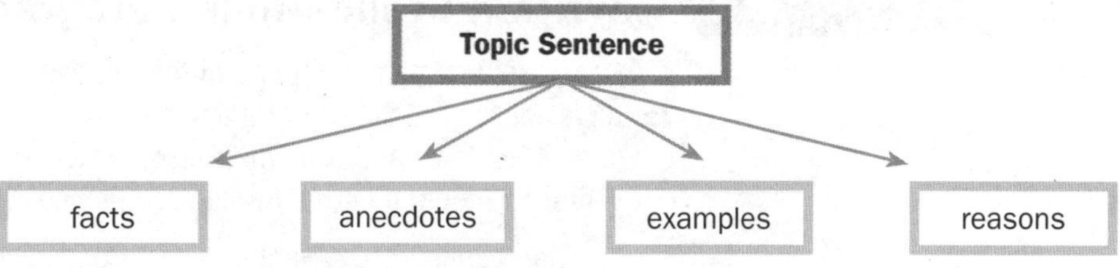

WRITING EXERCISE 3

Write three supporting ideas for each of the following topic sentences.

Example: I made several spending mistakes.

a. I bought a shirt that I never wear.

b. I paid too much for my car.

c. I bought a cellphone, but it is not as good as my old phone.

1 My class partner is very compatible with me.

a. ______________________________

____

b. ______________________________

____

c. ______________________________

____

2 We are very lucky to live in this country.

a. ______________________________

____

b. ______________________________

____

c. ______________________________

____

3 A good life includes the following elements.

a. ______________________________

____

b. ______________________________

____

c. ______________________________

____

COMPOSE IT

Write a Stand-Alone Paragraph

Compose a paragraph on one of the following topics or choose your own topic. Make sure that your paragraph contains a topic sentence and supporting facts and examples. Also, make sure that it is coherent. Every sentence should relate to the topic sentence.

Bad habits   Health   Consumer culture

Other topics: ______________________________

An **essay** is divided into three parts: an introduction, a **body**, and a **conclusion**. Look at the following example to see how different types of paragraphs form an essay.

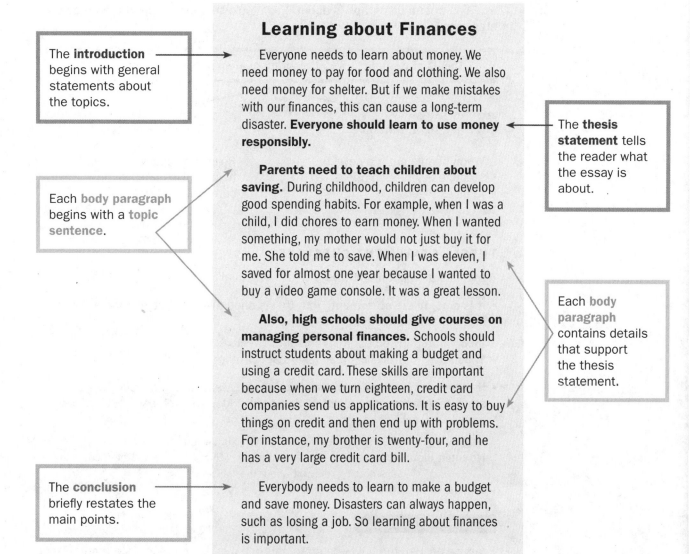

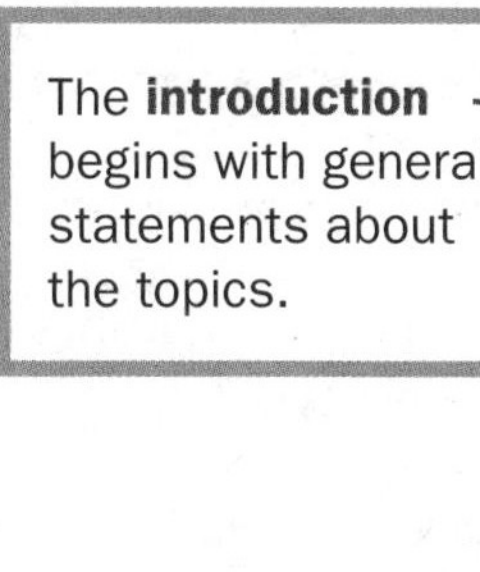

Learning about Finances

Everyone needs to learn about money. We need money to pay for food and clothing. We also need money for shelter. But if we make mistakes with our finances, this can cause a long-term disaster. **Everyone should learn to use money responsibly.**

The **thesis statement** tells the reader what the essay is about.

Each **body paragraph** begins with a **topic sentence**.

Parents need to teach children about saving. During childhood, children can develop good spending habits. For example, when I was a child, I did chores to earn money. When I wanted something, my mother would not just buy it for me. She told me to save. When I was eleven, I saved for almost one year because I wanted to buy a video game console. It was a great lesson.

Each **body paragraph** contains details that support the thesis statement.

Also, high schools should give courses on managing personal finances. Schools should instruct students about making a budget and using a credit card. These skills are important because when we turn eighteen, credit card companies send us applications. It is easy to buy things on credit and then end up with problems. For instance, my brother is twenty-four, and he has a very large credit card bill.

The **conclusion** briefly restates the main points.

Everybody needs to learn to make a budget and save money. Disasters can always happen, such as losing a job. So learning about finances is important.

The Introduction

The **introductory paragraph** introduces the subject of your essay. It helps your reader understand why you are writing the text. The thesis statement is the last sentence in your introduction.

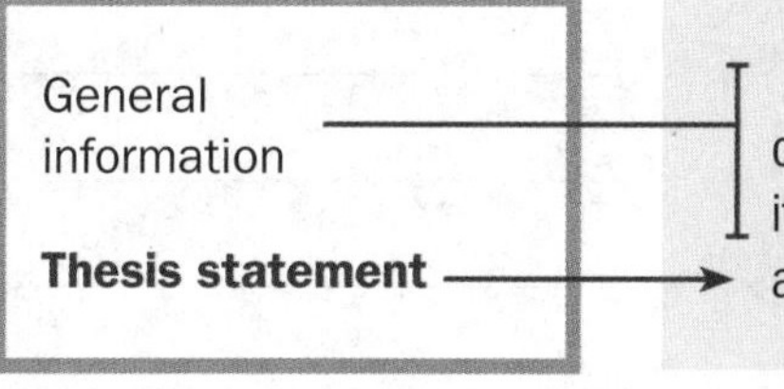

Canada is a materialistic nation. At a young age, children watch commercials about breakfast cereals and toys, and they learn to desire those items. In fact, the average child sees thousands of advertisements before the age of six. **Advertisers have too much influence in our culture.**

The Thesis Statement

The **thesis statement** is a sentence that expresses the main idea of an essay. Look at the following thesis statements.

Some video games promote violence.
To have a good life, we need strong relationships and an interesting job.

The **thesis statement** explains what the essay is about. A **topic sentence** explains what a paragraph is about. Each topic sentence supports the thesis statement.

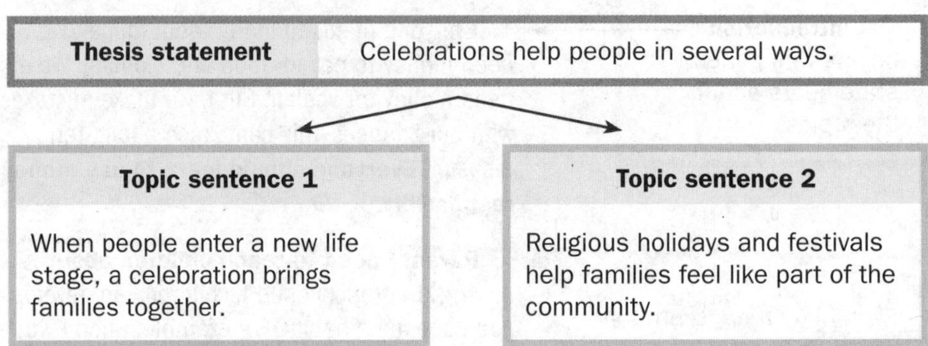

Thesis statement
Celebrations help people in several ways.
Topic sentence 1
When people enter a new life stage, a celebration brings families together.
Topic sentence 2
Religious holidays and festivals help families feel like part of the community.

THESIS STATEMENT CHECKLIST

A thesis statement must have the following qualities.

- **It is a complete statement.** Your thesis should have a subject and a verb and express a complete idea.

  Incomplete: The best things about travelling.
  Thesis: Travelling teaches us about other cultures.

- **It expresses a clear topic and a main idea.** Make sure that your thesis statement expresses a point of view or attitude. Avoid phrases such as *My topic is* and *I will write about*.

  Vague: I had a big problem. (The topic is unclear.)
  No main idea: I will discuss my car accident. (This sentence has no focus and says nothing relevant about the topic.)
  Thesis: My car accident changed my life.

WRITING EXERCISE 1

Examine each of the following statements. If it is a good thesis statement, write TS on the line provided. If it is not a good thesis statement, then identify the problem. Write *incomplete*, *vague*, or *no main idea* on the line.

Example: I will talk about driving. No main idea

People should not drink and drive. TS

1 The high cost of student housing. ____________

2 In this paper, I will discuss my job. ____________

3 Some musicians are very bad role models. ____________

4 The problems with tattoos. ____________

5 This changed my life. ____________

6 Art courses teach students important skills. ____________

WRITING EXERCISE 2

Write a thesis statement for each of the following groups of supporting ideas. Make sure that your thesis statement is complete and expresses a clear topic and main idea.

Example: Thesis: When you buy a car, make an informed decision.

a. Ask family members what type of car would be most useful.

b. Determine how much money you can afford to pay for the car.

c. Do research on the Internet about the specific types of cars that you are interested in.

1 Thesis: ______________________________

____

a. The park is often filled with aggressive dogs.

b. Also, in the park, there are broken bottles in children's play areas.

c. Furthermore, during the evenings, gangs meet in the park, and there are often fights.

2 Thesis: ______________________________

____

a. First, I do not smoke because I grew up in a household full of smokers, and I hated the smell of cigarettes.

b. Also, my grandmother died of lung cancer.

c. Finally, my best friends don't smoke, so I never felt pressure to develop the habit.

COMPOSE IT

Write Thesis Statements

Write thesis statements for two of the following topics, or choose your own topics. Remember to narrow each topic and to give it a specific focus.

Nature Celebrations Travel Technology

Other topics: ______________________________

Introduction Styles

You can introduce your essay in several ways.

- **General background:** You can write a few general sentences about the topic.
- **Historical background:** You can give some historical information about the topic.
- **Anecdotal:** You can tell a true story about something that happened. Your story should relate to the topic.

You end your introduction with the thesis statement, which expresses the main point of the essay.

WRITING EXERCISE 3

In the following introductions, the thesis statement is in bold. Decide what introduction style is used in each paragraph.

1 In the past, skateboards were not safe. The wheels were hard, and skateboarders had many accidents. In 1960, skateboarding became so dangerous that the sport lost popularity. But new inventions, such as rubber wheels and better bearings, made skateboarding a safer activity. **Skateboarding is an exciting and important sport.**

Style: a. General b. Historical c. Anecdotal

2 There are many ways to exercise. Every city has gyms and other sporting clubs. Information about healthy food is also easy to find. Food labels tell consumers about the sugar and salt in foods. **Some simple steps can help you to improve your health.**

Style: a. General b. Historical c. Anecdotal

3 Justin Bieber's mother put one of his songs on YouTube. Six months later, American music companies contacted the young boy from Ontario. Soon, he became an international star. **YouTube is having a large impact on the entertainment industry.**

Style: a. General b. Historical c. Anecdotal

COMPOSE IT

Write an Introduction

Write an introduction for an essay on one of the following topics, or choose your own topic. End your introduction with a clear thesis statement.

Nature Celebrations Travel Technology

Other topics: ____________________

The Supporting Ideas

In an essay, each body paragraph provides supporting evidence for the thesis statement.

Introduction
The **thesis statement** identifies the main idea of the essay.

↓

Body paragraphs
The **topic sentence** identifies the main idea in each supporting paragraph.

Facts | Anecdotes | Relevant quotations

WRITING EXERCISE 4

Read the following essay and do the following:

- First, underline the thesis statement.
- Then write a topic sentence at the beginning of each body paragraph. The topic sentence should sum up the main point of the paragraph in an interesting way.

Introduction

Many countries have English-speaking populations. The United Kingdom, Australia, New Zealand, and Scotland are just some of the places where English is the first language. Around the world, more than one billion people speak English as a second language. You should learn English for two main reasons.

Support 1

Topic sentence: ____

____

In many countries, people communicate with tourists in English. For example, in Mexico City, most hotel employees speak English. When I travelled to Greece and Germany, I used my English in restaurants and on trains. Even in China, people in the tourism industry learn to communicate in English.

Support 2

Topic sentence: ____

____

Many companies have offices across Canada and the United States. Employees may need to communicate with people in other offices. Also, even when a company is French or Spanish, the customers may speak English. For example, Sasha Jasyk works at a software design company in Quebec City. Sasha speaks French with his co-workers, but he must often speak English with American clients. Therefore, the ability to speak English properly can improve your position in a company, and it can make you a more valuable employee.

Conclusion

When you have a chance to learn English, take it seriously. Your English ability can help you in your travels and your career.

COMPOSE IT

List Supporting Ideas

Choose one of your thesis statements from the Compose It section on page 143 and then, on a separate sheet of paper, brainstorm a list of supporting ideas for your topic.

Example: Thesis statement: People travel for several reasons.

Supporting ideas:
- too much stress at work
- learn about cultures
- eat exotic foods
- try new sports and activities
- practise another language

The Conclusion

You can conclude your essay by rephrasing your main points. Then you can end with a suggestion or a prediction. The following conclusion ends an essay about cellphone etiquette.

Remind the reader of your main points.

End with a prediction or suggestion.

In conclusion, cellphone users do not show enough respect to the people around them. Their cellphone rings are annoying. They answer their phones in movie theatres and classrooms. Parents should teach their children about cellphone etiquette.

WRITING EXERCISE 5

Read the next paragraphs and follow these steps.

- Underline the topic sentences in body paragraphs 1 and 2. (Look for a sentence that expresses the main idea of each paragraph.)
- Then write an introduction. You can begin with an anecdote, historical information, or general information. End your introduction with a thesis statement.
- Finally, create a short conclusion.

Introduction: ______________________________

____

____

____

____

____

____

Body paragraph 1: First, students can save money when they live at home. Instead of working to pay for rent and food, students can concentrate on their studies. They won't accumulate debts. For instance, I live with my parents, and I have savings in the bank. When I finish college, I won't have any debts. My friends Gabriel and Antonio moved out of home to go to college, and they are always broke. On weekends, they rarely want to go out because they don't have enough money.

Body paragraph 2: Second, students who live at home do not have as many distractions as students who live in an apartment or dormitory. In college residences, there are often parties. People in other apartments make a lot of noise and listen to loud music. It is hard to concentrate on homework and on projects. For example, my two best friends got an apartment together. They never sleep during weekends, and now Gabriel is failing his college courses. So it is better to live at home.

Conclusion: ______________________________

____

____

____

____

The Essay Plan

A plan is a visual map that shows the essay's main and supporting ideas. It also includes details for each supporting idea.

Thesis statement: People travel for two main reasons.

1. **Topic sentence:** They need to get away and relax.
   Support: Maybe they have too much stress at work.
      Details: My parents work very long hours and they need a break.
   Support: They want to spend time with the family.
      Details: Our family went to the lake.

2. **Topic sentence:** They want to learn about other cultures.
   Support: They can practise a new language.
      Details: When we went to Cancun, we practised Spanish.
   Support: They can eat new types of food.
      Details: We loved the mole, tortillas, and other treats in Mexico.

Concluding suggestion: Everybody should travel to different places.

COMPOSE IT

Create an Essay Plan

Create an essay plan. Your teacher will give you a topic, or you can develop one of the topics from the Compose It section on page 144.

Introduction

Thesis statement: ______________________________

____

Body paragraph 1

Topic sentence: ______________________________

____

Support: ______________________________

____

Details: ______________________________

____

Support: ______________________________

____

Details: ______________________________

____

Body paragraph 2

Topic sentence: ______________________________

____

Support: ______________________________

____

Details: ______________________________

____

Support: ______________________________

____

Details: ______________________________

____

Conclusion

(Think of a final suggestion or prediction.) ______________________________

____

Revise for Correct Vocabulary

USING A DICTIONARY

Use a dictionary to ensure that your words are varied and correctly spelled.

1. Check your dictionary's features. Often, the preface contains explanations about various symbols and abbreviations. Many dual-language dictionaries contain lists of irregular verbs. See what your dictionary has to offer.

2. When you write a word in your paragraph or essay, make sure that you use the correct part of speech!

   Incorrect: I hope to become a veterinary.
   (Veterinary is an adjective.)

   Correct: I hope to become a **veterinarian**.
   (Veterinarian is a noun.)

WRITING EXERCISE 1

In each sentence, the underlined word contains a mistake. Look for spelling mistakes or incorrect word forms. Use a dictionary and write the correct words in the blanks. You can use an online dictionary.

Example: We past many summers at the beach. passed

1. In the past, people had strange believes about ghosts. ____________
2. During the comedy festival, I had funny. ____________
3. As a child, I was sometimes scary of the dark. ____________
4. Jason is a big spending. He buys everything that he wants. ____________
5. For exemple, he buys the most expensive cellphone. ____________
6. In many contries, people have celebrations. ____________

Revise for Adequate Support

In a paragraph, support your ideas with adequate examples. You can state facts or give examples from your life or from the lives of people you know. The following paragraph needs specific examples to make it more complete.

Paragraph without adequate support:

Countries have national holidays and celebrations for many reasons. Sometimes, the holiday marks a political or historical event. Many celebrations also have a religious component. Finally, certain celebrations are fun or romantic.

WRITING EXERCISE 2

Add details and specific examples to make the sample paragraph more complete and interesting.

Countries have national holidays and celebrations for many reasons. Sometimes, the holiday marks a political or historical event. ______________________
____
____

Many celebrations also have a religious component. ______________________
____
____

Finally, certain celebrations are fun or romantic. ______________________
____
____

Revise for Coherence

Your writing should be coherent. In other words, it should be easy to understand. Connections between ideas should be logical. You can use different words and expressions to help the reader follow the logic of a text.

Coordinators connect ideas inside sentences. Common coordinators are *and*, *but*, *or*, and *so*.

I love the winter, **but** I don't like driving in the snow.

Subordinators join a secondary idea to a main idea inside a sentence. Some common subordinators are *although*, *after*, *because*, *before*, *if*, *unless*, and *until*.

I love the winter **although** I hate cleaning the snow off my car.

Transitional words or phrases connect sentences and paragraphs. Common transitional words are *first*, *then*, *however*, *therefore*, *of course*, and *in conclusion*.

First, some people drive too fast.

WRITING EXERCISE 3

The examples listed below are words and expressions that are used to connect ideas. They illustrate different functions. Write a definition or translation beside any words that you do not understand.

Connecting Words and Phrases

Chronology (time)	first*	____________	next	____________
	second*	____________	suddenly	____________
	third*	____________	then	____________
	after that	____________	finally	____________

Addition	additionally also	____________ ____________	furthermore as well	____________ ____________
Example	for example	____________	for instance	____________
Emphasis	above all clearly	____________ ____________	in fact of course	____________ ____________
Contrast	although but on the other hand	____________ ____________ ____________	however or on the contrary	____________ ____________ ____________
Summary	to conclude in short	____________ ____________	therefore in conclusion	____________ ____________

*Do not write "firstly," "secondly," or "thirdly," etc. It is preferable to write "first," "second," and "third," etc.

WRITING EXERCISE 4

Read the following paragraphs. Underline the most appropriate transitional expression.

Most people think about their physical health. [1](However / Furthermore), they do not consider their emotional health. Levels of stress and depression are increasing. [2](In fact / Suddenly), in a recent survey, 25 percent of the respondents reported feeling anxious and tense. A certain amount of stress is normal and even positive. Stress can push us to create and explore. Excessive stress, [3](on the other hand / therefore), can cause severe health problems. Headaches, backaches, and nausea are connected to stress. [4](Furthermore / On the contrary), high blood pressure and heart disease may also be caused by excessive stress. [5](Therefore / Although), people should take actions to decrease their stress.

[6](Unless / Although) it is impossible to completely eliminate stress, there are some strategies that can reduce it. First, eat healthy meals and exercise. [7](Additionally / Because), take some time each day for uninterrupted relaxation. Meditate, listen to music, or just rest on the sofa. [8](However / In conclusion), take care of your mind and your body.

For more practice revising and editing writing samples, view the Revising and Editing sections at the end of chapters 1 to 7.

Here are some points to remember when you make an oral presentation.

Planning Your Presentation

- **Structure your presentation.** Make your introduction appealing. Use facts or examples to support your main points. Make sure you include a conclusion.
- **Practise.** Plan your presentation and recite it in front of a mirror several times. Your teacher will not be impressed if you pause frequently to think of something to say, or if you constantly search through your notes.
- **Do not memorize your presentation.** Simply rattling off a memorized text will make you sound unnatural. It is better to speak to the audience and refer to your notes occasionally.
- **Time yourself.** Ensure that your oral presentation respects the specified time limit.
- **Use cue cards.** Write down only keywords and phrases on your cards. If you copy out your entire presentation on cue cards, you could end up getting confused and losing your place. Look at the example provided.

Presentation Text
During my childhood, my parents gave me an allowance of $5 per week. I saved my money when I wanted to buy something, such as a video game. If I needed extra money for large items, I had to earn it by doing chores. I learned to save and be responsible.

Cue Card
allowance
$5 / week
video game
chores
save
responsible

Giving Your Presentation

- Look at your entire audience, not just the teacher.
- Do not read. However, you can use cue cards to prompt yourself during the presentation.
- When the assignment requires it, bring in visual or audio supports. These can help make your presentation more interesting.

What is your middle name? Do you have a nickname? Read the following definitions of names. Then answer the questions that follow.

Names

First name	▪ Given name	Example: *Robert*
Last name / Surname	▪ Family name	Example: *Bowland*
Maiden name	▪ Married woman's original family name	
Middle name	▪ Name that falls between the first and last name Example: Robert *Andrew* Bowland	
Nickname	▪ Shortened (familiar) form of a first name Example: "*Bob*" is short for *Robert*.	

Titles

Mr.	▪ Title before a man's name	Example: *Mr. Raoul Perez*
Miss	▪ Title before a single woman's name	Example: *Miss Lucy Ru*
Mrs.	▪ Title before a married woman's name	Example: *Mrs. Ellen Roe*
Ms.	▪ A woman's title regardless of marital status	Example: *Ms. Bella Smith*
Dr.	▪ Short form for "doctor"	Example: *Dr. Ramon Cruz*
Prof.	▪ Short form for "professor"	Example: *Prof. Martin Chin*

Marital Status

Single	▪ Not married
Married	▪ Legally united
Widowed	▪ Having lost a spouse (husband or wife) through death
Living common law	▪ Living as a couple but not married
Separated	▪ Living apart from a husband, wife, or domestic partner
Divorced	▪ No longer legally married

VOCABULARY EXERCISE

Elizabeth Anne Roland is a young woman. Her family and friends call her Lizzy. Last summer, she married a doctor named Richard Eric Blain.

1 What is the woman's first name? ______________________

2 What is her maiden name? ______________________

3 What is her nickname? ______________________

4 What is her middle name? ______________________

5 What two titles can Elizabeth use?

a. Mr. b. Mrs. c. Miss d. Ms.

6 What is Richard's surname? ______________________

7 What two titles can Richard use?

a. Mr. b. Mrs. c. Dr. d. Ms.

Days of the Week

Monday Tuesday Wednesday Thursday Friday Saturday Sunday

Days of the week always begin with a capital letter. (*I go to the gym every Friday.*)

The most commonly confused weekdays are Tuesday and Thursday. To help you remember, Tuesday is the second (number "two") day of the week.

Months

January	March	May	July	September	November
February	April	June	August	October	December

Months always begin with a capital letter. (*I was born in January.*)

Seasons

spring summer fall winter

Seasons always begin with a lower-case letter. (*I go camping every summer.*)

Dates

When you say a date, write *on* + MONTH + DAY.

The test is **on March 21st**. My birthday is **on January 3rd**.

In English, there are cardinal and ordinal numbers. Examine the differences between them.

Cardinal Numbers

1 – one	5 – five	9 – nine	13 – thirteen	17 – seventeen
2 – two	6 – six	10 – ten	14 – fourteen	18 – eighteen
3 – three	7 – seven	11 – eleven	15 – fifteen	19 – nineteen
4 – four	8 – eight	12 – twelve	16 – sixteen	20 – twenty

100 – one hundred 1000 – one thousand 1,000,000 – one million

Notice the difference between numbers that end in "teen" and "ty."
13 – thirteen 14 – fourteen 30 – thirty 40 – forty

Ordinal numbers can have different endings.

The following numbers end with the "st" sound, Example: 1st – first.

1st, 21st, 31st, 41st, 51st, 61st, 71st, 81st, 91st

The following numbers end with the "nd" sound, Example: 2nd – second.

2nd, 22nd, 32nd, 42nd, 52nd, 62nd, 72nd, 82nd, 92nd

The following numbers end with the "rd" sound, Example: 3rd – third.

3rd, 23rd, 33rd, 43rd, 53rd, 63rd, 73rd, 83rd, 93rd

All other numbers end with the "th" sound, Example: 4th – fourth.

4th, 5th, 6th, 7th, 8th, 9th, 10th, 11th, 12th, 13th, 14th, 15th, 16th, 17th, 18th, 19th, 20th

To practise your pronunciation, visit My eLab. You will find a variety of pronunciation exercises.

Pronunciation Rules

Review the pronunciation rules. Practice exercises appear in the chapters indicated. You can also visit My eLab to practise your pronunciation.

Present Tense: Third-Person Singular Verbs (Chapter 2)

Rules	Sounds	Examples		
Most third-person singular verbs end in an *s* or *z* sound.	**s**	works	hits	eats
	z	learns	goes	says
Add *-es* to a verb ending in *-s*, *-ch*, *-sh*, *-x*, or *-z*. Pronounce the final *-es* as a separate syllable.	**iz**	touches watches	reaches relaxes	fixes places

Past Tense: Regular Verbs (Chapter 4)

Rules	Sounds	Examples		
When the verb ends in *-s*, *-k*, *-f*, *-x*, *-ch*, and *-sh*, the final *-ed* is pronounced as *t*.	**t**	asked kissed	watched wished	hoped touched
When the verb ends in *-t* or *-d*, the final *-ed* is pronounced as a separate syllable.	**id**	wanted related	added folded	counted waited
For all other regular verbs, the final *-ed* is pronounced as *d*. Example: filled	**d**	lived killed	aged cured	moved played

Past Tense: Irregular Verbs (Chapter 4)

Rule	Sound	Examples		
When the verb ends in *-ought* or *-aught*, pronounce the final letters as *ot*.	**ot**	bought fought	taught brought	caught thought

Silent Letters (Chapter 6)

Rules	Silent Letters	Examples		
gn: For most words, when *g* is followed by *n*, the *g* is silent.	**g**	si**g**n desi**g**n	forei**g**n resi**g**n	beni**g**n Exception: signature
mb: When *m* is followed by *b*, the *b* is silent.	**b**	com**b** clim**b**	dum**b** plum**b**er	thum**b**

kn: When *k* is followed by *n*, the *k* is silent.	**k**	**k**now **k**nee	**k**new **k**nit	**k**not **k**nife
l: Do not pronounce *l* in some common words.	**l**	shou**l**d ca**l**m	wou**l**d ta**l**k	cou**l**d wa**l**k
t: Do not pronounce *t* in some common words.	**t**	lis**t**en Chris**t**mas	whis**t**le fas**t**en	of**t**en cas**t**le
w: Do not pronounce *w* in some common words.	**w**	**w**rite	**w**rong	**w**ho
gh: In some words, the *gh* is silent. (Note that in some words such as *laugh* and *cough*, *gh* sounds like *f*.)	**gh**	thou**gh**t li**gh**t	bou**gh**t thou**gh**	dau**gh**ter wei**gh**

Th **(Chapter 7)**

Rule	Sound	Examples		
To pronounce *th*, push your tongue between your teeth and blow gently.	**th**	think death	three moth	theatre breath

Pronunciation Help with Online Dictionaries

Many dictionaries are available online. On dictionary.reference.com, the stressed syllable is indicated in bold. By clicking on the loudspeaker, you can hear the word being pronounced. (Note that dictionary.reference.com also has a "Thesaurus" tab.)

co·op·er·a·tion [koh-op-uh-**rey**-shuhn]

From *dictionary.reference.com*

PRONUNCIATION EXERCISE

Use a regular or online dictionary to determine which syllable is accented in each word. Underline the accented syllable.

Example: rec<u>ep</u>tionist

1 laboratory
2 secretary
3 equitable
4 invent
5 inventory
6 happening
7 beginning
8 medicine
9 navigate
10 navigation
11 psychiatrist
12 cooperate
13 filtration
14 motivate
15 motivation
16 offered
17 preferred
18 happened
19 operate
20 operation

Alamy
p. 102: © Radka Linkova.

Bigstock
p. 20 top left centre: © Harveys Art; bottom centre: © Njari.

Canadian Broadcasting Corporation
p. 48: © Canadian Broadcasting Corporation.

Cauchi, Dan
pp. 99, 100.

crocosauruscove.com
p. 95 middle: © Tourism NT.

Flickr
p. 94 bottom: © Ricardo Hurtubia; p. 95 top: © Ravenshoe Group.

fotolia
pp. 1, 18: © Pavel_Markevych; p. 22: © vlorzor; p. 31: © rodjulian; p. 33: © Soloviova Liudmyla; p. 44: © Bert Folsom; p. 47 top right: © Sergey Bogdanov; bottom left: © javiindy; bottom right: © pio3; p. 50: © Patryssia; p. 61: © Todd Taulman; p. 64: © Monkey Business; p. 76 middle left: © Mariusz Blach; p. 78: © 5second; p. 87 top: © mark penny; p. 94 top: © vichie81; middle: © Sergey Nivens; p. 98: © vetal1983; p. 101 top: © Oleg Zabielin; bottom: © Gena; p. 106: © Serg Zastavkin; p. 107: © Morenovel; p. 118; © Photographee.eu; p. 121: © Focus Pocus LTD; p. 129: © momius.

iStockphoto
p. 20 top centre: © Tupungato; top right centre: © Mark Evans; top right: © Ragsac; bottom left centre: © Timurock.

Shutterstock
p. 2 top, left: © seprimor; top, right: © Nata Snobnikova; bottom, left: © Danie Nel; bottom, right: © Mukhina Viktoriia; p. 8: © Edyta Pawlowska; p. 11: © Pathdoc; p. 13 right, p. 81 top: © Maridav; p. 13 left, p. 93 right centre: © YanLev; p. 14: © Merkushev Vasiliy; p. 15: © Pierre Desrosiers; pp. 19, 37: © Ditty_about_summer; p. 20 top, left: © Tatiana Popova; bottom, right centre: © Boguslaw Mazur; bottom, right : © Lana K.; p. 21: © stockshoppe; p. 24 top, left: © wavebreakmedia; top, right: © aremar; middle, left: © racorn; bottom, left: © Photographee.eu; bottom right: © mkornflakes; p. 24 middle right, p. 117: © Sean Locke Photography; p. 25 top left: © Mi ti; top, right: © kitty; bottom: © S-F; p. 27 top: © Calin Tatu; bottom: © alphaspirit; p. 29: © Daxiao; p. 30: © Ollyy; p. 35: © Victor Tongdee; pp. 38, 55: © oneinchpunch; p. 39 top: © nito; bottom: © Pavel Burchenko; p. 40: © CROX; p. 42: © Stuart Miles; p. 45: © Andres Rodriguez; p. 47 top, left: © Alexander Image; p. 49: © Evan Lorne; p. 51: © Matthew Jacques; pp. 56, 74: © Lightspring; p. 58: © pleam; p. 62: © wong sze yuen; p. 66: © James Steidl; p. 67 top: © blydone; middle, left: © Piyato; middle, top centre: © MJTH; middle, bottom centre: © Jose AS Reyes; middle, right: © Nicotombo; p. 68: © Everett Historical; p. 71 top: © Jason Patrick Ross; bottom: © Fer Gregory; pp. 75, 91: © canadastock; p. 76 top, left: © Suwatchai Pluemruetai; top, right: © StockLite; middle, right: © aragami12345s; bottom, left: © Tyler Olson; bottom, right: © rj lerich; p. 77: © NOWAK LUKASZ; p. 79 top: © Bin Thanh Bui; bottom: © corbis_fancy; p. 80: © tisskananat; middle: © Carlos Yudica; bottom: © Sabphoto; p. 82 top: © Chris102; middle, right: © STUDIO GRAND OUEST; middle, left: © Angela Hawkey; bottom: © stockyimages; p. 86 top: © everst; bottom, left: © rdonar; bottom, centre: © Galyna Andrushko; bottom, right: © Vladimir Kogan Michael; p. 87 bottom: © claffra; p. 89: © Andrea Izzotti; pp. 92, 111: © Photobac; p. 93 left: © Joe West; left centre: © riteski goce; right: © Ammit Jack; p. 95 bottom: © Migel; p. 96: © Steve Mann; p. 103 top: © DJTaylor; bottom: © CURAphotography; p. 105: © EmiliaUngur; pp. 112, 131: © aabeele; p. 114: © igor.stevanovic; p. 115 left: © vierra; left centre: © JK 1991; right centre: © Shell114; right: © Umberto Shtanzman; p. 116: Denis Vrublevski; p. 119: © Milles Studio; p. 123: © bikeriderlondon; p. 124: © luckytonyom; p. 125: © Photosani.